CONTENTS

Whether You're a First-Time Home Builder or an Experienced Contractor...

...Design America's exceptional home plans and helpful, knowledgeable staff will make your project a complete success!

♦ ♦ ♦

1 Choose the Design America Home Plan Book that offers plans for the style of home you've always wanted.

The plans in our Design America Series have been created by many of the nation's top architects and designers. No matter what your tastes, you're sure to find several homes you would be thrilled to call your own.

You can select from a wide range of styles, including the hottest new trends in contemporary styling. Design America has them all! We also showcase outstanding plans of affordable homes for those who are building on a budget.

In addition to more than 200 home plans included in each Design America book, you'll find a wealth of other helpful information. Companion articles will give you hints on securing construction financing and show you how easy and inexpensive it is to customize your plans.

Order a complete set of blueprints.

Design America plans provide you with a complete blueprint package from as low as **$195.00. Blueprints include the following:**

• Exterior elevations of all sides

• Foundation plans and details

• Scaled floor plans

• Locations of electrical outlets, switches & light fixtures

• Plumbing schematic plan (If available)

• Roof & wall sections

• Cross-section view

• Material list and general notes (If available)

It's reassuring to know that Design America's blueprints meet one or more nationally recognized building standards at the time and place they were drawn. If you'd like a preview of one of our home designs, ask us about a Preview Plan of the home. Some plans offer a Preview Plan that shows the exterior elevation drawings of the plan, the floor plan, and kitchen cabinet elevations.

Customize the blueprints you select for a tailor-made home just for you.

From changing siding material to adding a walk-in closet or a room, our design staff will save you thousands of dollars over what you might otherwise pay. For a nominal charge, we can even mirror-reverse the entire plan!

In addition to design customization, Design America also provides assistance in securing construction financing. **Call us today** and we'll be happy to give you more information on this helpful, time saving service.

Our #1 goal is to help you build the home that matches your needs and lifestyle.

Call us toll free **(800) 533-4350** or fax us your blueprint order today at **(800) 344-4293.** Let's get started on your new home!

Real Life Home-Building Experiences

Are you wondering what it's like to build your own home?

Let those who have gone before you share what they have learned.

◆ ◆ ◆

If you're apprehensive about tackling such a huge project as building your own home (and who wouldn't be?), take heart. People of all levels of experience and backgrounds have successfully built homes for themselves. There are many ways to achieve your goal of a custom-built home. If you wish to avoid as many headaches as possible, hiring an experienced builder to handle all the details is the answer. If you possess a lot of confidence and have the desire to save as much money as possible, acting as your own general contractor is the way to go. There are even those who use a blended approach, hiring a builder to take care of some tasks, and completing the rest themselves. In all cases, the key to success is to do your homework. Doing the proper research first helps to minimize problems down the road. Part of that research is understanding the mistakes others have made so you can learn from them.

Playing the Role of the General Contractor

When you are the general contractor on your home building project, you can expect to have more challenges to deal with than if you hire a builder. Those who have lived through the experience have learned, however, that the snags aren't insurmountable. Sometimes these challenges can be turned into positives and **you can save a lot of money.**

Chuck Weidner, of rural Harvard, Ill. is a repeat customer of National Plan Service USA,Inc. Twenty years ago he used plans from NPS to build a home in suburban Chicago. In April 1993 he and his wife Annette, following a set of Design America plans, started construction on another home situated on ten acres near the Wisconsin state line. They chose the design, a truly grand Victorian home encompassing over 2,500 square feet with an enormous porch that wraps around more than half of the house. Chuck and Annette are proof that you can play the role of general contractor if you're willing to endure some difficulties. Together, they served as the general contractor on both homes.

Other than five years working in construction (he's a police officer now), Chuck had no experience as a general contractor prior to building the first home. He and Annette taught themselves as they went through the process. What was the most trying part of the whole experience? "Making sure that all the subcontractors got their work done on time," answers Chuck. "Personality conflicts between the subcontractors was the biggest challenge. For example, the carpenters weren't happy with the way the electrician's were doing their work. The sheetrock was delivered at the same same the insulators were here, and it caused some difficulties...you just need to talk to both of them and make some compromises."

Chuck and Annette had the misfortune of buying their lumber shortly after Hurricane Andrew hit southern Florida in the fall of 1992. The demand for lumber for rebuilding caused prices to skyrocket. "The first time we went for bids was in September," explains Chuck, "and then we didn't really finalize it until January or February. The price of just the lumber went up $12,000...that was something we did not plan on."

Despite these problems, work progressed smoothly. The Weidners didn't need to alter their house plans to get the village's approval. There were no construction delays, even for the weather, and the project was completed on schedule. The solution to one particular problem turned out to augment the design of their house. The excavators and laborers were having trouble installing the septic tank because of the slope of the ground. "They had to move the house 15 or 20 feet," explains Chuck, "and that raised the foundation in the back where we now have a walk-out basement."

Chuck & Annette Weidner

Weidner Residence   Photo courtesy of Carl Cullen

When you are your own general contractor, finding a construction loan can also be difficult. Banks are hesitant to lend if an experienced builder isn't involved. "We looked at a few banks," says Chuck, "but they all wanted to see a builder." The Weidners eventually financed the construction of their latest home with a home equity loan taken out on their old house.

"The most enjoyable part of the whole experience was seeing everything coming together," says Chuck, "Towards the end, when all the goodies come in such as the trim, cabinets, and flooring...then it starts looking like a house." Another positive outcome was the money Chuck and Annette saved by not hiring a builder. They **estimate their savings totalled $40,000.**

Would he recommend that anyone try being a general contractor? "I would say yes. With a little guidance from someone that's in the trades who knows what the difficulties are...I think anybody can do it." What advice would he give someone who's considering such an undertaking? "Make sure you're working with reputable people, get several bids, and check with the county where you get your permits, because they can make helpful recommendations (when looking for subcontractors)." Chuck mentioned that negotiation skills are also helpful when dealing with the trades.

Obviously, if asked if they would do it again, Chuck and Annette's answer would be

yes. And, they would use Design America plans. The Weidners were so impressed with the quality of the plans and service they received that they have recommended Design America plans to other people.

Hiring A Builder

Serving as your own general contractor involves managing all aspects of your home-building project. Building materials must be ordered, and competitive bids must be solicited. A complete work schedule must be created, and deliveries and subcontractors' work must be coordinated. In addition, you have to make sure that the subcontractors (or trades as they are also known) get paid on time so that no mechanic's liens are put on your property. Make sure the necessary building permits and insurance are in place, and it's your responsibility that the plans for your house get approved by the village building authority.

If this sounds too overwhelming, consider hiring a local builder to do this work for you. The builder will take care of as much of the project as you want. If you decide to hire a builder, finding a reliable one is essential. How do you go about finding a reputable builder? And what separates the good builders from the bad ones?

"Word of mouth is the best way to find a builder," says Eric Rossi of Avanti Construction Corp., a builder based in the near west suburbs of Chicago. Rossi has been in the business for 20 years and builds 10 to 15 houses per year in Chicago's western and northwestern suburbs. He recently used a set of Design America plans for one of his homes and was very pleased with the result. "Talk to people. See some spec homes. Go in and see the type of work their doing. Talk to people who have bought their homes and ask them what they think of their house," Ross recommends.

There are various third party sources that you can check out as well. Local attorneys and county offices should be able to provide you with information about the track record of a particular builder. Reporting services such as Dun & Bradstreet can be consulted as well. One especially important item to investigate is whether or not the builders pay their subcontractors on schedule. A sub who doesn't get paid on schedule can place a mechanic's lien on your property preventing you from calling it your own until he gets paid. Every builder has had to fend off mechanic's liens at one time or another, however, the fact that a builder has a few doesn't necessarily mean he isn't doing his job. "That's one of the problems in the business," says Rossi. "Any guy that has a dispute can throw a lien on you. There should be some guidelines, there should be some standards that they have to meet, But there's nothing like that." A builder with many liens from several different subs should raise a red flag. A good builder will avoid all but the most frivolous liens. "I don't let things slide. My tradespeople perform and they get paid, and that's important," Rossi states.

It's a good idea to research and hire your builder early, while you're still in the planning stages, and even before your house plans are finalized. This is important because the builder will offer many helpful suggestions concerning the plans and specs. When it comes time to start construction, the builder may know of a more efficient or cost-effective way to achieve a certain result. The builder can also tell you if there are going to be any problems getting the village's approval for the plans. Good builders will always be doing research and attending trade shows to stay informed on the latest issues in the industry. You should tap into this knowledge as early in the process as possible.

Rossi points out that if your home's interior will be completed during the colder months, your labor costs will be less. This is because less construction takes place during the winter and so there are more plumbers, electricians, etc. available. With more trades competing for fewer jobs, they'll be more likely to offer discounted rates during winter.

Builders such as Rossi have built homes for many people and are full of helpful hints. Rossi recommends locating your financing first, before doing anything else. "The first thing to do is to find out what you're qualified for. You don't want to be looking for a $300,000 home if you've only qualified for $170,000. Then your next step is to find your land." Rossi recommends finding a lot in a location you like and then picking out house plans that fit the lot. Don't select your plans before the lot, and allow enough time for construction. "You've got to figure six to eight months to build a house even though everybody wants it in three," says Rossi.

The best piece of advice that Rossi can give to those building their own home is to choose your builder carefully. Shop around and select a builder based on reputation and the quality of their work.

It's Definitely Worth Building Yourself to Get Exactly What You Want.

Having owned half a dozen different houses and condos, Bob and Judy Sipek decided to build a custom home in a southwestern suburb of Chicago. Bob works as a project manager and Judy is a building manager. "We wanted a new home and so we found a lot we really liked in a nice subdivision and started looking for house plans and a builder," explains Bob. "We ended up going with the builder who built my sister's house because I could see he did quality work. I had been talking to various people and had a ballpark figure of what it would cost. This builder's price was in the ballpark. We knew his work and he could start right away so we went with him." In addition, their builder had built other homes in the same subdivision, and was familiar with local building codes and soil conditions.

The Sipeks chose the NP1348 Chesterton design from the Design America series. A contemporary design, the Chesterton features 1,890 square feet of living area neatly packaged into 1 1/2 stories. The home was built on a 1/4 acre lot. "We started looking at

Sipek Residence

Photo Courtesy of
Lewellyn Studio

plans about one year before we broke ground," says Bob. "The first plans we chose were from a company in Texas. But then we found out that the plans weren't certified for Illinois and it would've been very costly to modify them to comply." The Design America staff was able to deliver plans certified for Illinois and also incorporated some changes the Sipeks wanted to make. Among other things, they enlarged the first-floor master bath and rearranged some closet space to allow a first-floor powder room to become a third full bath. The Sipeks were somewhat pressed for time, but the Design America staff was able to meet their needs. "The company was good at rushing our changes through in about a week," says Bob.

This was Bob and Judy's first attempt at building a home for themselves, and they enjoyed the experience. Their greatest concern was finding a builder they could trust who wouldn't run into financial trouble during construction and be unable to finish. This concern wasn't great enough, however, to cause them to try their hand at being a general contractor.

The only real problem the Sipeks encountered was a time crunch towards the end of the project. There were some rain delays, and a rather complicated roofline took longer to construct than anticipated. Bob and Judy had to wait an extra six weeks to move in, but delays such as these are common. In fact, allowing enough time for construction is one piece of advice the Sipeks offer first-time home builders. They started researching plans and builders about one year in advance of construction, but really could have used a year and a half. It's also important to match the design of your home with your lifestyle. "When you pick out a floor plan, think about how you live," says Judy. "Since we don't have kids, I wanted every place I need most to be on the main floor, and the rooms that we don't use all the time somewhere else. This house fits just perfectly."

Even with the construction delays and minor problems, the Sipeks agree that building their custom home was well worth it. Neighbors are always saying how much they

like the house and Bob and Judy couldn't be happier. **"It's definitely worth building yourself to get exactly what you want**," says Judy. "We plan to retire here."

Make Design America Plans Part of Your Home-Building Experience

Many people have built their own custom homes and so can you! Allow enough research time, solicit bids from a variety of builders or subcontractors, insist on quality work, and choose Design America plans. By following these tips from successful home builders, you'll be well on your way to living in that home you've always wanted. Design America also offers books on building and construction to help you start your project with a solid foundation of knowledge.

Analyze the Blueprints Before Building to Create the Best Possible Home of Your Dreams

Article by Guhner-Jahr Publishing
Build-It & Build-It Ultra

There need be nothing "stock" about a custom home built from pre-drawn mail-order plans. In fact, with imagination and/or professional guidance, thousands of homeowners have modified existing blueprints to create truly personal, character-filled homes. Changes can range from simple facade embellishments, such as articulated door and window casings, to major spatial modifications—for example, combining two small bedrooms to create a grand master suite with a bath and dressing room.

Though dramatic in effect, many custom touches may not even require new architectural drawings. Other, more substantial changes are best accomplished with the help of an architect or other design professional, who can prepare any new drawings that are needed.

In either case, it is critical to consider and decide on any changes early in the process, long before construction begins. Otherwise, any bids you solicit prior to changing the plans will be inaccurate. Worse still, if you ask for modifications during construction, your project is likely to be beset by delays and cost over-runs.

Material Choices

Among the simplest changes are those related to materials. Let's say your plans and specifications call for clapboard siding, but you prefer the more rustic look of wood shakes. Simply select the alternative material, change the specification, and you've personalized your home-to-be. Other easy-to-change materials with a potentially big impact on a home's looks include roofing and the trim around windows and doors.

One step further are changes that affect both materials and design. For example, many two-car garages are designed with a single, large door, but you may prefer the lighter look of two single-width doors. Or, instead of the double-hung windows in the plans, you may opt for the more gracious look of floor-to-ceiling casements.

In many instances it's possible to "test" the visual impact of such changes by sketching in the alternate materials on tracing paper laid over the elevations in the blueprints. These changes should not be treated lightly, however, and if you're unsure, it's a good idea to invest in some professional design help. (For more on the importance of material specifications, see "Specifying Your Dream." page 14.)

Floor Plan Changes

Another area to consider is the floor plan itself. Though today's mail-order house plans are generally well-designed with the needs of modern families in mind, it's often possible to make a change or two in the layout that turns an almost-perfect design into an ideal home for your family. Removing a single wall, for example, might create the large, open living room/dining room you desire. Or, raising the garage's walls and roof by just 4 feet could turn an unfinished storage loft into the spacious home office you need.

Kitchens and baths, which are the most complicated and most used rooms in the house, deserve special attention. A luxurious two-person shower, for example, may better suit your lifestyle than a standard tub/shower combination. Similarly, an expanded kitchen

Article Courtesy of Guhner-Jahr Publishing.

CUSTOMIZE IT !

Small changes on paper can greatly improve your plans, but make sure you decide on any modifications before construction begins.

◆ ◆ ◆

that can accommodate two sinks and dishwasher may be the perfect solution if you entertain frequently.

Again, you can begin by sketching your ideas on tracing paper laid over the blueprints. If you can't figure out the layout changes needed, seek professional advice from an architect or other design professional.

Working with Pros

If you're confident about the changes you desire but can't quite visualize or draw them, you can hire an architectural draftsperson—perhaps a local architecture student—who can turn your ideas into finished plans and/or elevations. Rates for drafting start at about $25 per hour.

If you need design help or advice about materials—especially if you're considering changes that will affect the house's structure, such as moving or removing walls—seek the services of an architect or other qualified design professional. Registered architects are trained to address both spatial and structural questions. Designers vary more in training and experience; some are best at what was traditionally called decorating, while others are fully adept at space planning.

Many architects and designers will work on an hourly consulting basis, with fees ranging from about $75 to $125 per hour or more, depending on professional accreditation, experience and location.

Kitchen and Bath Specialists

Kitchens and baths are highly specialized design areas, so make sure whatever type of design pro you choose has a lot of experience. One option is to seek out a Certified Kitchen Designer (CKD) or Certified Bath Designer (CBD). To earn this title, professionals must meet special requirements, pass tests and obtain certification from the licensing arm of the National Kitchen & Bath Association

(NKBA). In addition to providing design services, CKDs and CBDs can help you select and can provide materials and products for the kitchen and bath.

Kitchen and bath dealers, many of whom are NKBA members, work out of showrooms that sell cabinets, appliances, bath fixtures and more. Most dealers provide design services and provide products and materials.

A Custom Home Doesn't Have to be Expensive

It's true. If you're planning on building your next home, it's cheaper to customize your own design and hire your own builder than it is to choose a plan from a large developer who's building a subdivision. Even if you accept the developer's stock plans with no modifications, it will still cost you more than building a custom home from your own plans. And the home need not be large, either. No matter if your dream is for 1300 or 3000 square feet, you'll spend less by designing and building yourself.

Why it Makes Sense to Build Your Own Custom Home

You might be thinking, "But how can that be? Can't those big developers build houses cheaper because of the volume of business they do? Don't they get volume discounts on their building materials?" That might be the case, but they also incur significant costs associated with marketing their developments.

It's easy to see these marketing expenses when you take a look at a new subdivision. Consider the model homes that are built for prospective home buyers to tour. The developer has to pay for the interior designers who decorate the homes as well as for all the custom furnishings and landscaping. The salespeople who work there seven days a week must also be paid. Costly brochures promoting the subdivision must be created, and advertising space in newspapers and on television and radio must be purchased. The developer can recoup some of these expenses when the models are sold, but not all of them because the models are sold at a discount. Much of the cost gets passed on to you, the buyer, making the homes more expensive. By building yourself, using custom plans, you can avoid paying those extra costs and have a more personalized home, too!

What's the Best Source for Customized Plans?

You could hire an architect to draw up your custom plans, but you may end up spending thousands of dollars to get the design you want. A better alternative is to purchase customized plans from Design America and spend only hundreds. Design America has top-quality plans, and the expertise and the willingness to back them up with good customer service. Since we've been designing people's dreams for over 80 years, we know what you're looking for in a home. And because of the volume of our business, we can offer customized plans at prices that are 25 – 50% less than what a professional designer would charge.

Even if your future home is less than a mansion, you'll save money by building yourself with custom plans from Design America

◆ ◆ ◆

Example of plan modification

Rendering courtesy of Select Home Designs   **FIG 1**

Revised Plans after modifications   Photo courtesy of Select Home Designs

plans yourself. After all, we're the architects! We'll do the sketching; you just tell us what you want changed. After we evaluate your request, we'll estimate how much the changes will cost **free** of charge and how long they will take. Of course, price and lead time will vary depending on the extent of the modifications.

NPS Can Provide Your Plans in Several Different Formats

If you won't be making any changes to the stock plans you've selected, then you should order your plans in the form of blueprints. Blueprints are non-erasable and non-reproducible so not even minor changes can be made to them by you or your builder. Order these only if you're sure nothing else will be altered. You'll probably need 4 – 7sets for everyone involved in the construction of your new home. You'll want one set for yourself, of course. The village or local government body that's responsible for approving the design will need a set. Your lender will request plans before a loan is approved, and finally, the general contractor will probably need several sets for all of the subcontractors.

If you want to make only very minor changes, ones the contractors can make themselves, then you should order plans that are reproducible. These plans can be erased and redrawn. If you only want to move a wall a few feet or enlarge a walk-in closet, these plans allow the contractor to erase lines and redraw them. Mylar, vellum plans are also reproducible, so you can make as many copies as you need for all the parties involved. Because mylar, vellum plans are reproducible, they are slightly more expensive than blueprints.

The Customization Process

The first step is to browse through our Design America Series and select the design that comes closest to your idea of a perfect home. Design America has hundreds of different designs to choose from. If the simplified drawings and renderings in our plan books give you enough information, then fax us your request for changes. Just let us know what changes you need as outlined preceeding page (pg.11, fig.1) and our architects will do the rest.

If you'd like to buy a set of plans first, Design America's helpful design staff will discuss any customization options with you at the time of your order. Feel free to ask as many questions as you like. If changes are necessary, you can tell us at the time of your order. Preferably, you should give us the modifications in writing via mail or fax so there is no confusion over any of the details.

Other home plan companies may ask you to mark up a diagram of the home with the desired changes. But NPS believes you shouldn't have to worry about drawing your

The Design America Advantage:

Other home plan companies' service will stop after you've received your modifications of the plans. They'll redraw the plans and send them off to you. But what happens if the village authorities won't approve construction because your plans don't meet local codes or ordinances? This can be a serious problem. And the fewer problems you have when building a house, the better. What good are plans for a home that can never be built? With other plan companies, you're on your own, but not with Design America.

We realize that local building codes may be complex. Our plans are drawn to meet one or more national standards. Sometimes this isn't enough, however. Regional and local authorities often have their own sets of codes that must be met. If you're building in a subdivision, the seller of the lots may impose certain building restrictions or covenants that must be followed. In some cases, you may not fully understand the codes, or some restrictions may get missed. Design America will help you wade through all of this bureaucracy and help you get your plans approved.

"We realize that the homeowner may not be well versed on the technical aspects of dealing with all of the different codes and ordinances," says David Azran, President of National Plan Service USA, Inc. "We see ourselves as being a liaison between the homeowner and the builder. If permitted, we'll actually sit down with the homeowner and builder and discuss what has to be done to get the plans approved." If your plans are questioned by village authorities because of code requirements, Design America will get in touch with the village and find out exactly which parts of the plans need clarification. Then we discuss what must be done with you and make the changes needed to earn the village's approval.

One of Design America's customers recently learned the value of this **exceptional service** when a conflict arose concerning the topography of the customer's lot. The local authorities rejected the homeowner's plans because the village felt the home's design was not compatible with a small hill on the site. The builder contended there was no hill, but the village insisted there was. After numerous discussions with the builder and the village, Design America discovered the problem. The village was using out-of-date drawings, and there really was no hill!

Peace of Mind With Your Customized Plans

We're sure you can see the value of Design America's services. This peace of mind is included in the price you pay for your customized plans. So call Design America today, at **(800) 533-4350** and let us assist you in the construction of your new home.

The More Active Your Role in Selecting Materials, Products and Techniques, the Better Your Home

Article by Guhner-Jahr Publishing
Build-It & Build-It Ultra

The best custom homes are carefully tailored to meet their owners' needs and wishes, and nowhere is this more important than in the selection of products, materials and construction techniques. After the workmen leave and you move in, the home will be a complete success only if you're pleased with the wood, glass, metal and stone used to transform your blueprints into a house.

Of course, many of the physical elements that comprise a home are spelled out in floor plans, elevations and allied documents. But some of these specifications may be generic, meaning there are still decisions to make. And even when a specific item is listed, you may prefer a different option—perhaps in-floor radiant heating rather than the forced hot-air furnace shown in the blueprints, or oak interior doors instead of pine.

Though it may seem easier to leave all these details to the contractor, the fact remains that you will live with the results, maybe for a lifetime. So the investment you make now in learning about the options will pay handsome dividends for years. Here's what to consider and how to find information and assistance.

Upgrade from plastic laminate to granite kitchen counters, for example, and your house may cost $7,500 more. Specify floor-to-ceiling ceramic tile in the baths instead of small tiled areas around the tub, and the additional cost might be $3,000 – $5,000, depending on the specific tile you choose.

Naturally, your total budget for the construction of the house will help to determine your material and product selections. The important point is to consider the many options—and their costs—early in the planning stages, ideally before putting your plans out to bid. That way the fixed price you contract for will reflect the many materials, products and techniques you want for the home, rather than choices the contractor may have made to save time and increase his profit.

If you're ready to solicit bids, but haven't made final decisions on every material, tell the contractors to exclude those elements from their prices. Or, if you have a good idea of what you're willing to spend on, say, flooring, ask them to include a flooring allowance of that dollar amount.

Dollars and Sense

One of the best reasons to take an active role in product and material specification is to maintain budgetary control over your project. Obviously, the various options in each product category related to the home carry widely differing price tags, and those costs go directly to your home's bottom line.

Rendering courtesy of Alan Mascord Design Associates

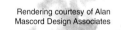

Rendering courtesy of Alan
Mascord Design Associates

Filling in the Blanks

Another key concern is to fill in the blanks on all specifications that are treated generically in your plans. Though a complete set of blueprints, materials lists and specification sheets represents a comprehensive set of instructions for building a home, it does not necessarily provide a single choice for every detail.

For example, plans may call for "hardwood flooring" without indicating the type of wood or pattern to use. Or they may indicate the size and position of appliances and plumbing fixtures, but not the brands or model numbers. The same may be true of siding, roofing, windows, heating and cooling equipment, cabinetry, door hardware, even such final details as switchplates. In the end, someone must make the decision between inexpensive knotty pine clapboard and top-quality cedar, or between brand X appliances in black versus brand Y finished in stainless steel. And, taken together, these choices will have a profound impact on what becomes your home. Rather than accept someone else's choice, consider the options available in each instance and select the one that best satisfies your needs, desires and budget.

Upgrades

Even when items are listed specifically in the plans, it's worth analyzing the choices and considering upgrades. In roofing, for example, premium asphalt shingles not only look better than standard products, but also carry 50 percent longer warranties, making them a good value over time. Energy-efficient high-performance window glazing offers similar benefits when life cycle costs are factored in, as do top-quality cabinets built to last for decades.

Other changes relate more to aesthetics, but are just as valid. If you've always wanted goldplated bath fittings, why pay for chrome-plated models? Likewise, if standard-issue oak strip flooring is not your dream for a living room, it makes little sense to pay for it now only to switch to polished maple in a few years. Want classic ceramic mosaics on the bathroom walls? Specify them now rather than remodeling later.

Construction Techniques

The techniques used by a contractor to build your home can greatly affect its quality and the amount of maintenance and repairs you'll face over the years. Though your selection of an experienced, competent builder takes care of much of this question, there are some details worth specifying if you want top quality. Here are some important ones that may or may not be listed in your existing spec sheets:

• Drywall should be affixed with screws, rather than nails, which are more likely to pop. Skim coating all ceiling and wall surfaces

*Article Courtesy of Guhner
-Jahr Publishing*

with joint compound produces a better looking, more plaster-like finish than simply taping the joints between drywall sheets.

• Vapor barriers should be affixed to studs and joists prior to drywall to prevent condensation in wall cavities.

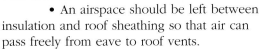

Rendering courtesy of Alan Mascord Design Associates

• An airspace should be left between insulation and roof sheathing so that air can pass freely from eave to roof vents.

• Sills, the horizontal wood members on top of foundation walls, should be cut from pressure-treated lumber so you'll never have to worry about rot.

• Valleys, rakes and eaves—the most vulnerable parts of a roof— should have a waterproof membrane applied under flashing or shingles.

• Wood siding and exterior trim that will be painted should be back primed prior to installation; this will extend the life of a paint job.

• Interior and exterior painting should include a primer and two finish coats, which can outlast a single coat by as much as 50 percent.

Information and Assistance

The specification of products, materials and techniques is a complicated business. But the task becomes much easier if you familiarize yourself with the available options.

You should also shop local lumberyards, home centers, kitchen and bath dealers, lighting stores, etc., to see and price the possibilities. Collect manufacturers' product literature and scour design magazines for ideas as well. If it's a book you're after, we recommend "The Apple Corps Guide to the Well-Built House," by Jim Locke, Houghton Mifflin, 1988.

If you'd rather spend your money than your time, consider an architect or other design professional on a consulting basis. Working from your budget and preferences, a pro can prepare a detailed spec list for your approval, can analyze a list you've prepared and suggest worthwhile changes, or can present you with a range of good options.

However you proceed, if your aim is the best, most personal custom home possible, make sure work doesn't begin until there's a complete materials list and specification sheet that you understand and with which you're comfortable. Otherwise, you may have to start planning a remodeling soon after you move in.

✍

Financing the Construction of your Custom Home

by Kevin D. Woodard

Even before you have finalized the plans and site for your new custom home, your thoughts should turn to answering the question, "Where am I going to get the money to fund construction?" Unless you have large sums of cash saved up, you will need to take out some sort of loan to allow construction to begin. A conventional mortgage loan is not the answer at this stage, because you don't yet have a house to mortgage. For some, a home equity line of credit on their existing house can provide the cash they need. For most people wanting to build their own home, however, a *construction loan* is necessary. A permanent mortgage (also known as an *end loan* or *take-out loan*) will come later. This may sound unfamiliar to you, so let's go through the loan acquisition process one step at a time.

1. Select the source of financing

Professionals in the lending industry suggest looking to your current bank first for construction financing. You and your bank are familiar with each other, and the loan officers might already have a good idea of your present financial condition. Banks love to have multiple deposit and lending relationships with their customers and that is a good bargaining chip to have when you are negotiating the terms of your loan. But be forewarned: most banks will not lend to you if you are acting as your own general contractor unless that is how you make your living. Experience in the construction business is everything from the bank's point of view, so plan on hiring an experienced builder to oversee the construction for you unless you have a proven track record as a general contractor.

Other financial institutions can serve as funding sources as well. These include mortgage banks and brokers, and your company pension or savings plan. Retirement plans are often good for providing construction money because of the favorable terms at which you can borrow against your accumulated funds. Another source of funding is the builder himself. Your builder has a revolving line of credit with his bank and can use that to finance the construction of your new home. This arrangement simplifies things because you don't have to go to the trouble of applying for a loan at a bank. But there are disadvantages. A large deposit will be required up front and the interest the builder pays on his credit line will, of course, be passed on to you. You would pay this interest yourself anyway if you were borrowing directly from the bank, but then you would get the benefit of a tax deduction. When looking for possible sources of financing, rely on those who really know the business. Ask real estate attorneys, realtors, and local builders if they can recommend a lender.

2. Determine the type of loan that is best for you

Construction loan plus end loan. This is the most common way to finance the construction of a new home. With this arrangement, you actually get two separate loans to cover your financing needs: one for the construction phase and one for the "live in" phase after the home is built. The construction loan finances all costs associated with

Photo courtesy of Design Basics, Inc.

Photo
courtesy
of Select
Home Designs

building the house. The end loan is nothing more than a conventional mortgage that pays off the construction loan. The construction loan typically has a term of six months to a year and is an "interest only" loan. This means your monthly loan payments include only interest calculated on the amount that you have borrowed. None of your payment goes toward reducing the principal balance. The principal balance is never reduced during the entire term of the construction loan. The interest rate you pay is usually tied to the prime rate and is stated as so many points over prime. The "spread" over prime can be anywhere from 1 to 2 percentage points. The rate will fluctuate as the prime rate fluctuates and may adjust monthly or even daily. Make sure you understand exactly how and on what amount the interest is calculated.

As described below, the loan proceeds are metered out in stages. It's obviously better for the interest payments to be calculated on only that portion of the loan amount that has actually been disbursed. You don't want to pay interest on money that is not even being used yet.

Expect to pay some points when you close on your construction loan. Points are a percentage of the loan amount that must be paid up front. One point equals 1 percent. For example, a one point fee on a $100,000 loan would be $1,000. The lender charges points to cover various expenses associated with administering the loan. It's important to note that these points are not like the optional discount points you can pay on a conventional mortgage. Points on a construction loan are a pure fee for the lender and do nothing to reduce your interest rate. They typically range from 1 to 2.5 points. More points are charged on construction loans than on mortgages, because construction loans are more costly to administer. As an incentive to

stay with the same lender for your permanent mortgage, some institutions will let you use .5 point as a credit towards any points you pay on the mortgage.

A down payment will, of course, be required. Lenders usually require at least 20 percent down. This equates to a loan-to-value ratio (LTV) of 80 percent. Don't expect to get your entire loan amount disbursed to you all at once. In fact, you won't actually see any of the money at all unless you are acting as your own general contractor. The funds will be distributed to the general contractor in increments called "draws." The institution advances each draw when a specified stage of construction has been completed. For example, money will be advanced when the foundation is laid and when the framing goes up. A title company usually takes care of the actual disbursements. A representative of the lender or title company will usually inspect the project before each draw to verify that the work is being completed as planned. In addition, you the borrower may be required to sign off on each completed stage before a draw is made.

After the construction phase, when your new home is ready to be occupied, you're ready to take out the end loan. The end loan can come from the same lender as the construction loan or from a different lender.

Combination loan. Unlike the scenario presented above, in this case one loan takes care of all the financing. At the end of construction, the construction loan is simply converted into a permanent mortgage. This can save you money on closing costs since you only have to close once. Of course, you must use the same institution for construction and permanent financing.

Home equity loan. If there is a lot of equity built up in your present house, a home equity line of credit could be used as a construction loan. Equity credit lines usually have minimal paperwork and lower costs associated with them. Up to 80 percent of your home's market value may be available to use for construction financing.

3. Gather information and documents required at the time of the loan application

Here is a list of items that lenders typically require you to provide at the time you fill out a loan application:

Sworn contractor's statement. This document itemizes the contractor's estimate of all costs associated with building your home. It also lists who the subcontractors are and what they will do. It is signed by the general contractor.

General contractor's information letter. This is a form that the lender asks the builder to complete. It asks the general contractor questions about experience, insurance, bonding, etc. It helps the lender evaluate the general contractor.

Detailed blueprints and specs. The bank or other lending institution doesn't want to lend more than about 80 percent of the estimated value of the completed home. Blueprints and specs are needed for making this estimate of market value.

Signed contract between the builder and the individual. This proves you have an experienced builder working for you. It also assures the lender that the house will be built.

Deed to your lot. The lender will not grant you a loan without first knowing that you own the land on which your home will be built. If the lot is mortgaged, you will also need to have on hand all of the relevant loan documents.

Personal financial information. These are the standard items commonly required by all mortgage lenders and serve to verify your income, expenses, assets and liabilities. You'll be required to provide W-2s, paystubs, previous addresses for the past two years, name and address of employer, information on bank accounts, and outstanding loan balances, etc.

4. Close on the loan and start construction

Just as in a closing for a permanent mortgage, there are costs associated with closing on a construction loan. In addition to the points mentioned earlier, there will be recording fees, attorneys' fees, notary fees, etc. Costs such as these can vary from lender to lender, so it's a good idea to compare points and fees when shopping for a construction loan.

It's a lot of work finding construction financing and evaluating all of the options. But it will all be worth it as you watch your custom home take shape.

To help you evaluate your different financing options, Design America now offers a financing referral service. Call Design America today at **(800) 533-4350** to find out more about this new time-saving service.

Photo courtesy of
Select Home Designs

A Wealth of Information When You Decide To Build Your Own Home

Now that you've decided to build your own home and have picked the plans ...where do you go? With today's home improvement market booming, you, the consumer, have more choices then ever before. Below are some helpful hints.

LUMBER YARDS

Materials, materials, materials ..How much do I need? ...How much will they cost?...What grade of lumber should I purchase? **Your local lumber dealer is the place to start.** Here you will find a service or lumber desk. The people behind that counter just may be your next best friends. You'll typically find estimators on hand who can provide a "take off", in other words an estimate, from your blueprint or materials list. This will be based on the grade of materials that you specify. Their estimates are typically right on target. Remember that they are in the business of selling lumber. Thus you will find them both helpful and attentive because they want your business.

Although don't expect them to do it while you wait; they usually are working on numerous sets at any given time. This is especially true in early and middle spring when the majority of housing starts take place.

HOME CENTERS

Huge stores, miles of products, and helpful staffs. Although you may be overwhelmed by its sheer size you can find practically anything here. Today's typical home centers can be over 100,000 square feet with full service garden building centers. Here you get both discounted prices and idea centers. These stores have everything for home improvement and more.

You ramble past full kitchen and bath displays, order custom blinds, browse through thousands of different wall paper patterns and borders.

HARDWARE STORES

Here is the place to go when things get down to the nitty gritty or you need speed and convenience. When your stuck on a pipe fitting or need specialized fasteners your local hardware store will help you. Hardware store are the one retail outlet where a local and community atmosphere exists. Employees here will help you answer the most difficult questions and help you find the most distinguished nuts and bolts.

A Quick Guide so You'll Know What to Expect Once Construction Begin

N ow that you've settled on your plans, the joy of turning your dreams into reality begins in earnest. The wrenching matter of financing needs to be settled, and a patch of land selected. Such decisions can take weeks or even years, depending on your determination and sometimes your luck. But once the time comes to break ground, a house can't be built fast enough.

Constructing a home can take anywhere from six months to one year (or more), depending on a number of factors. The size of the house, number of workers, weather conditions and unexpected—but inevitable—delays, all make a difference. Though the order of work may vary slightly and local building inspection requirements differ, this timetable, spread over a seven-month period, will give you a sense of what to expect and when.

Rendering courtesy of
Alan Mascord Associates

Months 1 & 2

- Municipal and state permits obtained
- Site work and excavation
- Pour foundation
- Building inspection of foundation
- Frame floors
- Rough-in electrical and plumbing under floors
- Inspection of rough-in mechanical systems if house is built on slab
- Install first floor subfloor

Months 2 & 3

- Frame walls, roof and ceilings, including all door and window rough openings
- Install remaining subfloors
- Apply exterior wall and roof sheathing
- Rough-in remaining electrical and plumbing lines in wall, ceiling and floor cavities.

Months 3 & 4

- Building inspection of mechanical rough in and exposed structural work
- Apply roof flashing and shingles or other roofing material
- Install windows and exterior doors
- Apply exterior trim (window and door casings, fascia)

- Apply exterior wall finish material (i.e., clapboard, vinyl siding, stucco)

Months 5 & 6

- Install cabinets and countertops
- Apply ceramic tile in baths
- Finish plumbing and electrical work (light switches and fixtures, outlets, install sinks, tubs, etc.)
- Painting and wallpapering
- Install finish flooring

Months 6 & 7

- Install appliances
- Install hardware
- Inspection by homeowner and final touch-up work
- Site cleanup and landscaping
- Final building inspection
- Final payment to contractor
- Move in!

*Article Courtesy of
Guhner-Jahr USA Publishing*

Design America Designers

National Plan Service USA, Inc.

(The publisher of the "Design America" house plan book series)

With a history that dates back to the early 1900's, when it offered do-it-yourself plans to lumber dealers, and individual consumers, the motto of National Plan Service USA, Inc., has become "Turning Your Dreams Into Reality For Over 80 Years."

Based in Bensenville, IL, the in-house staff of registered architects and designers at NPS work to provide consumers with unlimited design possibilities. These designs range from starter homes to luxury designs, with many alternatives to fit virtually any home-building budget. Home plans from NPS can easily be modified to suit a buyer's particular needs and lifestyle. The company offers customization services, as well as general advice and assistance to make the experience of building a new home as pleasurable as possible.

Many NPS designs reflect the regional influences of the northeast and midwestern United States. These solid, time-proven designs incorporate feedback from the thousands of customers who now live in homes built from fully detailed blueprint packages provided by NPS.

DESIGN BASICS, Inc.

Design Basics, Inc. creates home plans for builders nationwide. The company markets its plans, which are designed for single family dwellings, through catalogs and trade publications. The company originated in 1983 when its primary purpose was to design plans for custom home builders in the metropolitan areas. Seeing danger in controlling too much of the local market, the company's focus shifted from designing custom home plans locally to designing plans that were adaptable anywhere. Included in these plans is a construction license allowing the purchaser to build the plan as many times as desired, and a promotional license granting the right to produce the camera-ready art work for promotional purposes. Today, Design Basics is nationally recognized through numerous awards, not only for their designs, but also for achievements in business management, corporate growth, sales, and the development of effective marketing

products. This growth and success, in turn, has helped Design Basics, Inc. define their mission statement, "Bringing People Home." All the design products and services as well as each employee are a part of a culminating effort to help people attain their dream home.

CARMICHAEL AND DAME

It was 1986 when two small-volume builders, Patrick Carmichael and Robert Dame, merged their efforts and began designing and building homes for Houston's upper-end housing market. Carmichael's forte was in finance and business management; Dame's was in translating buyers' ideas into exquisite designs. The blend of their natural talents led them to their design/build firm, Carmichael and Dame. In 1994, with more than 300 designs accumulated, Carmichael and Dame made the decision to market designs nationwide by teaming up with Design Basics, Inc. one of Americas leading home plan design firms.

Carmichael and Dame plans are nothing meticulous, averaging 20-35 pages in length with specifications as detailed as the dimension of every piece of moulding. Unlike most plan services, each of the designs have been built by its own building division, ensuring the structural soundness and buildability of each plan as a result, Carmichael and Dame is able to provide builders and consumers with both technical and construction support throughout the building process. In addition, elegant watercolor renderings are available for each of their designs, as well as a Contract Development package - a complete materials specifications and quantities reference guide. Through itsr products and designs, Carmichael and Dame hope to rekindle the passion for excellence. "One of my dreams is that the craftsman aspect of design will return to the building industry in America as it was before the turn of the century," Dame says. "Our company has tried to do that by providing designs and products with a higher level of detail, craftsmanship, architectural significance and quality."

ALAN MASCORD DESIGN ASSOCIATES, INC.

Founded in 1983, Alan Mascord Design Associates, Inc. has developed an outstanding reputation in the industry for providing innovative, buildable stock plans. Mascord first began working with local builders, providing them with great plans for their projects. Soon it became apparent that these homes could be marketed nationwide;they began a direct mail program to reach builders in other areas. This success led to publishing opportunities and soon the company's plans were being featured in several national magazines.

Always interested in providing the best possible plans available, Mascord has wholeheartedly embraced the Computer Aided Design (CAD) technology. Starting in 1986, everything Alan Mascord Design Associates, Inc. has drawn has been on CAD. This has greatly improved the quality of its drawings and the efficiency of the drafting staff. Mascord, a professional member of the A.I.B.D. and the National Association of Home Builders, has been designing homes for 25 years. "In addition to projects all over the country, many of our homes have been built in Japan by the Mitsui Company, one of the biggest builders in Japan," says Mascord.

MICHAEL E. NELSON AND ASSOCIATES, INC.

At Michael E. Nelson and Associates, Inc. creativity, craftsmanship and technology are combined to form a unique offering in the home plan industry. By utilizing computer-aided drawing technology, Michael E. Nelson and his staff produce accurate and complete designs for individuals, designers and home builders throughout the United States, producing quality designs for over ten years. Michael E. Nelson & Associates' blend of creativity and technology has brought the firm recognition through several national publications and from the American Institute of Building Designers.

A constant quest for customer satisfaction has driven Nelson and Associates to produce a portfolio of plans that meet the needs of a diverse marketplace. The vast collection of plans range from traditional to contemporary, and can be modified to suit the special needs of clients. This collection of plans brings years of experience and insight together to form an invaluable resource to home builders and individuals alike.

VAUGHN A. LAUBAN DESIGNS

Vaughn A. Lauban Designs was established in 1976 incorporating Southern traditional and Creole farmhouse styles into its designs, Vaughn A. Lauban Designs has flourished. The company's home style developed a national market with its "Back to Basics" designs. With stock plans in demand in all 50 states and sev-

eral foreign countries, Vaughn A. Lauban purchased a small office building, expanded, and remodeled it to reflect this Early American feeling. "We still concentrate on the farmhouse designs, although now with additional designers on staff, Midwestern and European designs are drafted to satisfy a demanding market,"

says Vaughn A. Lauban.

SELECT HOME DESIGNS

With nearly 50 years of experience delivering top-quality and affordable residential designs to

the North American housing market, Select Home Designs is proud to continue that tradition. Since the company's inception in 1948, more than 350,000 new homes throughout North America and overseas have been built from Select Home Design plans. The Select Home Design team, however, is never content to rest on its laurels, and is constantly striving to develop the best new plans for today's lifestyles. With an outstanding collection of proven plans, virtually every architectural style and influence is represented, many featuring the latest design innovations: lavish master bathrooms, dramatic foyers, unique staircase designs, and generous use of outdoor living spaces such as decks, porches and patios. One of the most important features of a Select Home Designs plan is the flexibility it offers- which is always an important factor to consider when building a new home.

FILLMORE DESIGN GROUP

Fillmore Design Group was formed in

1960 by Robert L. Fillmore, president and founder. Over the years, the firm has grown to 12 designers and draftspeople. Fillmore designs are often characterized by their European influences, massive brick gables and high flowing, graceful roof lines". We spend considerable time on detail, particularly brick detail, and we often place a fireplace with decorative brick patterns along the front facade for focus and interest. In fact, this attention to detail extends inside the home and pays off in terms of handsome, finely wrought moulding, cornices, and other interior detailing," says Fillmore. "Each plan is done in our office by one of our experienced designers under close supervision and is checked and rechecked for accuracy before leaving the office," explains Fillmore. "Each plan is carefully thought out, down to the smallest detail by our design group. We pay attention to such items as traffic flow, open rooms with tall ceiling heights and window openings, while at the same time think of

furniture placement and wall space. We try to allow plenty of storage areas, large kitchens with good work patterns, luxurious and exciting master baths and spacious master bedrooms." Fillmore Design Group belongs to the American Institute of Building Designers and the National Association of Home Builders. The company's work has been featured in various national publications.

How To Work With An Interior Designer

The preliminaries

People hire interior designers for a variety of reasons. Some people realize that they don't have the skill or imagination to handle the job. Others don't have the time. And still others want an image - "drop-dead" chic, slick contemporary, or "instant-heritage" traditional. They hire a designer known for a particular look who can help them achieve the image they want.

A good interior designer is an interpreter who translates your *tastes* and needs into an environment that is comfortable, functional, and pleasing to look at.

The specifics

Shortly after agreeing to work with you, the designer will probably draw up a contract.

Although there is no set system of fees in the interior design business, most designers charge clients in one of several ways, or in combination:

By the hour: Some designers charge by the hour when the job is small. Others charge by the hour regardless of the scope of the job.

Flat fee: Usually arrived at based on the extent of the work and the amount of time the designer gauges it will take to complete the job.

Percentage: Some designers charge a percentage of what the total job - concept, labor, and materials - will cost, usually 20 to 30 percent, as their design fee.

Mark-up: If not charged hourly, services will be included in the retail price.

It is the designer's responsibility to come up with a plan that fits your budget. If the estimates for the job come in higher than the original budget, it's up to the designer to rework the design so that it stays in line with the amount you originally intended to spend.

Your role

Realize that the interior designer is one of the last custom professionals. The dressmaker, milliner, and bootmaker have all vanished. But the interior designer continues to produce custom one-of-a-kind design work. Custom work takes time.

You should also be aware that the interior designer is an intermediary. He or she relies on a fleet of other professionals - painters, upholsterers, and specialized craftsmen - to get the job done. Foul-ups do occur. The sofa may get delayed at the upholsterer's. The painter may get backed up in his work schedule. The custom-dyed fabric that was supposed to be delicate peach could arrive in bright orange. Be prepared for setbacks.

You can sit passively by and let the designer choose everything for you. But, if you get engaged in the process, it will be much more exciting. Most designers welcome the client who shows an active interest as the transformation takes place. Working with the designer to select accent pieces, accessories, and antiques is the best way to become involved in the process, since it allows you to add your personality to the environment the professional is creating. And it's a sure way to be entirely satisfied with the final look of the room.

Carol J. Guess, ISID

Please, Help Us To Help You

In order to ensure that our Design America series best serves your needs, please assist us by filling out the questionnaire below. As a token of our appreciation, we'll send you a **FREE CATALOG** of **Project Plan Ideas**. (Please check the correct responses.)

1. Is this book your
   - ❏ 1st home plan book
   - ❏ 2nd home plan book
   - ❏ 3rd home plan book
   - ❏ _____ plan book

2. What prompted you to buy this Design America book?
   - ❏ Number of plans offered
   - ❏ Various plan styles
   - ❏ Customization
   - ❏ Looking for building ideas
   - ❏ Book category
   - ❏ Helpful articles

3. How long have you been searching for your dream home plan?
   - ❏ 0 - 6 months
   - ❏ 7 - 12 months
   - ❏ 12 - 24 months
   - ❏ More than two years

4. Would you like information on financing your dream home?
   - ❏ Yes
   - ❏ No

5. Are you looking for land to build on, if so, where?
   - ❏ Yes _____
   _____

6. When do you plan to begin construction of your new home?
   - ❏ 0 - 6 months
   - ❏ 6 - 12 months
   - ❏ Within 2 years
   - ❏ Not sure, gathering materials

7. How much do you plan to spend on materials on your new home (excluding land)?
   - ❏ Less than $100,000
   - ❏ $100,000 - $149,000
   - ❏ $150,000 - $199,000
   - ❏ More than $200,000

8. What style of home do you plan on building?
   - ❏ Traditional ❏ Multi Family
   - ❏ Colonial ❏ Country
   - ❏ Contemporary ❏ Vacation
   - ❏ Ranch ❏ Victorian
   - ❏ Other _____

9. What additional information could we provide that would make it easier for you to build your dream home? (Please check all that apply)
   - ❏ Rear elevations
   - ❏ Interior elevations
   - ❏ Colored photographs of the homes
   - ❏ Approximate cost to build
   - ❏ More articles related to the home building process.
   - ❏ Other_____

10. Are you a . . . ?
   - ❏ Consumer ❏ Building Trades
   - ❏ Professional Builder/Contractor

11. In what type of residence do you currently live?
   - ❏ Single family home ❏ Townhouse
   - ❏ Condo / co-op ❏ Apartment
   - ❏ Other

12. The population of the city, town you currently reside?
   - ❏ less than 20,000 ❏ 83,000-100,000
   - ❏ 21,000-41,000 ❏ 101,000- +
   - ❏ 42,000-82,000

13. What is your gross annual household income - before taxes?
   - ❏ Under $30,000
   - ❏ $31,000 - $60,000
   - ❏ $61,000 - $80,000
   - ❏ $81,000 - $100,000
   - ❏ $101,000 +

Mail or fax to: NATIONAL PLAN SERVICE USA, INC., 222 JAMES ST., BENSENVILLE, IL 60106

NAME _____
ADDRESS _____
CITY _____
STATE_____ ZIP_____ PHONE (____) _____

PLEASE FAX TO   **1-800-344-4293**

Design America
Your Blueprints For Success

Our Blueprint Package contains nearly everything you need to get the job done properly and accurately, whether you're acting as your own general contractor or with help from an architect, designer, builder or subcontractors. Each Blueprint Package is the result of many hours of work by licensed architects or professional designers.

ACCURACY & QUALITY

Our staff of architects and professional designers have developed blueprints to ensure accuracy and quality.

VALUE

Purchase professional quality blueprints at a fraction of their development cost. With Design America, your dream home plan is attainable.

PROMPT SERVICE

Once you've chosen your dream home plan, fax your order to 1-800-344-4293 or call toll free at 1-800-533-4350. Upon receipt of your order, we will process it quickly!

SATISFACTION

With over 80 years of quality service to home plan buyers; past, present, and future, our experience and knowledge have made us a premier home plan company.

ORDER TOLL FREE
1-800-533-4350 or Fax 1-800-344-4293

After you've chosen your home plan package, simply mail or fax the accompanying order form on page 33 or call toll free on our Blueprint Hotline: 1-800-533-4350. We're ready to assist you in building your dream home.

- **HOUSE SECTIONS**
- **DETAILED FLOOR PLANS**
- **EXTERIOR ELEVATIONS**
- **INTERIOR ELEVATIONS**
- **FOUNDATION PLANS**
- **COVER SHEETS**
- **MATERIAL LIST**

Each set of blueprints is a collection of floor plans, exterior & interior elevations, details, cross-sections, diagrams and general notes showing precisely how your house is to be constructed.

Your Plans Will Show:

Cover Sheet

This artist's sketch of the exterior of the house, done in perspective, gives you an idea of how the house will look after it is built. This is only an artistic conception and may vary from actual working drawings.

Exterior Elevations

Drawn in 1/4-inch or 1/8-inch scale show the front, rear and sides of your house. General notes on exterior materials and finishes. A generic site plan may be incorporated in your blueprints.

Foundation Plan

Drawn to 1/4-inch scale, this sheet shows the complete foundation layout including support walls, excavated and unexcavated areas, if any, and foundation details. Specify slab construction, basement, or crawl when ordering.

Detailed Floor Plans

Completed in 1/4-inch scale, these plans show the layout of each floor of the house. All rooms and interior spaces are carefully dimensioned and keys are provided for cross-section details given later in the plans. The positions of all electrical outlets and switches are incorporated in this sheet.

House Sections

Large-scale cut-away views, normally drawn at 3/8-inch or 1/2-inch equals 1 foot, show sections or cut-away of the foundation, interior walls, exterior walls, floors, and roof areas. Additional cross-sections are given to show important changes in floor, ceiling or roof heights or the relationship of one level to another. Extremely valuable for construction, these sections show how the various parts of the house fit together.

Interior Elevations

These large-scale drawings show the design and placement of kitchen and bathroom cabinets, laundry areas, fireplaces, bookcases and other features. Little "extras," such as mantelpiece and wainscoting drawings, plus moulding sections, provide details that give your home that custom touch.

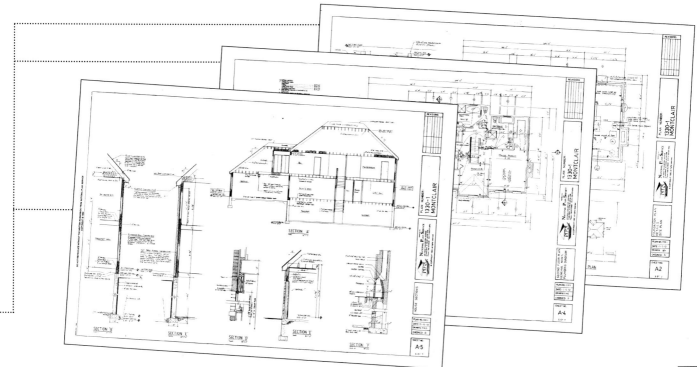

Design America Options and Services

Reversed

As Shown

Reversed Plans

Have you ever thought you've found the perfect home plan only the garage or porch is on the wrong side? The solution to this problem is in reversed, or "mirror image" plans. We can send one full set of "mirror image" plans (although the text will appear backwards) as a master guide for you and your builder.

Modifying Your Design America Home Plan

If you are considering making major changes to your design, we strongly recommend that you purchase our reproducible vellums and use the services of a professional designer, architect or ask our Design America staff. For this valuable service please call **1-800-533-4350 Architectural Dept.**

Our Reproducible Vellums and Mylars Make Modifications Easy

With a reproducible copy of our plans, a design professional can alter the drawings just the way you want. You can print as many copies of the modified plans as you need. And, since you have already started with our complete detailed plans, the cost of expensive professional services will be significantly less. Refer to the price schedule for vellums and mylars.

Don't Forget To Order Your Materials List

Our material list can help you save money. Available at a modest additional charge, the Materials List provides the quantity, dimensions, and specifications for the major materials needed to build your home. You will get faster, more accurate bids from your contractors and building suppliers. Materials Lists are available for most home plans, and can only be ordered with a set of plans. Due to differences in regional requirements and homeowner or builder preferences; electrical, plumbing and heating/ air conditioning equipment specifications are not designed specifically for each plan.

Financing Your New Home Program
Questions? Call our mortgage specialist at **1-800-533-4350**

Interior Design Services

Looking for the right image for your new home? We can help you with the right interior design image for your new home! Call our interior design expert at **1-800-533-4350**

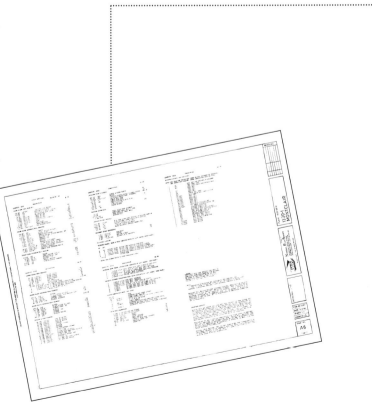

How Many Sets Of Plans Will You Need?

Single-Set Package

We offer this set so you can study the blueprints to plan your dream home in detail. Please NOTE that the Plans in this publication are copyrighted, therefore the plans cannot be reproduced. **Ignoring Copyright laws can be a costly mistake.**

The Standard 4-Set Construction Package

- First set is for yourself.
- Second set is for your builder.
- Third set is for your village or municipality.*
- Fourth set is for your bank.

The Contractor 7-Set Construction Package

- First set is for yourself.
- Second set is for your builder.
- Third set is for your village or municipality.*
- Fourth set is for your bank.
- Fifth set is for a plumbing contractor.
- Sixth set is for a heating contractor.
- Seventh set is for additional bids.

Generic Details for the Home Builder

Because local codes and requirements vary greatly, we recommend that you obtain drawings and bids from licensed contractors to complete your mechanical plans. However, if you want to know more about techniques— and deal more confidently with subcontractors—we offer these remarkably useful detail sheets. Each is an excellent tool that will enhance your understanding of these technical subjects.

Residential Construction Details

Eight sheets feature the essentials of stick-built residential home construction. Detailed foundation options - poured concrete basement, concrete block, or monolithic concrete slab. Shows all aspects of floor, wall, and roof framing. Provides details for roof dormer, eaves, and skylights. Conforms to requirements of Uniform Building code or BOCA code.

$14.95 each

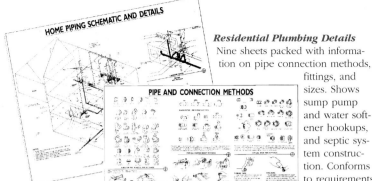

Residential Plumbing Details

Nine sheets packed with information on pipe connection methods, fittings, and sizes. Shows sump pump and water softener hookups, and septic system construction. Conforms to requirements of National Plumbing Code. Color coded with a glossary of terms. **$14.95** each

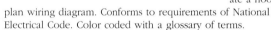

Residential Electrical Details

Nine sheets that depict all aspects of residential wiring, from simple switch wiring to the complexities of three-phase and service entrance connection. Explains service load calculations and distribution panel wiring. Shows you how to create a floor plan wiring diagram. Conforms to requirements of National Electrical Code. Color coded with a glossary of terms.

$14.95 each

Detail Plan Prices

Purchase any two (2) sets for only $22.96 or all three (3) for $29.97. See the Order Form on page 33.

Important Shipping Information

Your order is processed immediately. Allow 10 working days from our receipt of your order for normal UPS delivery. Save time with your credit card and our "800" number. UPS must have a street address or Rural Route Box number—never a post office box. Use a work address if no one is home during the day. Please call for international shipping information.

AN IMPORTANT NOTE:

1) All plans are drawn to conform to one or more of the building industry's major national building standards at the time and place they were drawn. However, due to the variety of local building regulations, your plan may need to be modified to comply with local requirements—snow loads, energy loads, seismic zones, etc. We strongly recommend that you consult with your local building officials or local architect for required information on submission of permit documents.

2) Detail plans are generic and do not conform specifically to the house plan that you purchase.

*Multiple sets of documents (blueprints) may be required by your local village or municipality building depts.

1. **Choose your Design America Plan**

2. **Would you like to customize your blueprints to your family's needs and lifestyle?**

   If YES: Talk to one of our blueprints experts at 1-800-533-4350 or in Illinois 630-238-0555

   If NO: Order the design number indicated at the top of the page, determine number of sets needed and specify if you are ordering a plan with foundation options; basement, crawl space, slab, pier.

3. **Upon having made your decision as to the design you wish to purchase, we recommend you order them through the Lumber yard, Home Center, or Hardware dealer who provided you with this book. Your local Lumber yard, Home Center, or Hardware dealer can give you valuable information and suggestions on you new dream home. Or mail, phone or fax us your blueprint order or customization request and we will process your order quickly. For accurate processing of your order please enclose check, money order, cashiers check or Master card/Visa information with the plan design number and order form (Page 33) To:**

NPS Design America, Inc.
Slot A-1
P.O. Box 66973 **DA 1000**
Chicago, Illinois 60666-0973
Ph. 1-800-533-4350 • 630-238-0555
Fax 1-800-344-4293 • 630-238-8885

Blueprint Prices

The cost of having an architect design a new custom home typically runs from 4 to 10 percent of the total construction cost, or from $4,000 to $10,000 for a $100,000 home. A single set of blueprints for the plans in this book ranges from $195 to $720, depending on the size of the house. Working with existing drawings may save you enough money on design fees to enable you to build a deck, upgrade your materials, or design a luxurious kitchen. Please note : garages, porches, decks, and unfinished basements are not included with the total living area, unless noted.

What will it cost to Build?

As noted in one of the articles, it is best to find out how much you can qualify for prior to building. Building cost vary widely from region to region, depending on a number of factors, including local material availability and labor costs, and the finished materials selected.

Foundation Options & Exterior Construction

Depending on your site conditions and region, your home will be built with a slab, pier, pole, crawlspace, or basement foundation. Exterior walls will be framed with either 2 by 4's or 2 by 6's, determined by structural and insulation standards in your area. Consult with your local building official in your area. Most contractors can easily adapt a home to meet the foundation and/or wall requirements for your area.

Service & Blueprint Delivery

Blueprint representatives are available to answer questions and assist you in placing your order. Plans are delivered via U.S. Mail or UPS.

Returns & Exchanges

Blueprints are specially printed and shipped to you in response to your specific order, consequently, requests for refunds cannot be honored.

Local Codes & Regulations

Because of climactic, geographic, and governmental policies set by your municipality, building codes and regulations vary from one area to another. These plans are authorized for your use only on the expressed consent that you oblige and agree to comply with all local building codes, ordinances, regulations, and requirements, including permits and inspections at time of construction.

Architectural & Engineering Seals

With increased concern about energy cost and safety, many cities and states require that an architect or engineer review and "seal" a blueprint prior to construction. To find whether this is a requirement in your area, contact your local building department.

License Agreement, Copy Restrictions & Copyright

When you purchase your blueprints, you are granted the right to use these documents to construct a single unit. All the plans in this publication are protected under the Federal Copyright Act, Title XVII of the United States Code and Chapter 37 of the Code of Federal Regulations.   Each designer retains title and ownership of the original documents. The blueprints licensed to you cannot be used by or resold to any other person, copied, or reproduced by any means. The copying restrictions do not apply to reproducible blueprints. When you purchase a reproducible set of mylars or vellums, you may modify and reproduce it for your own use.

AN IMPORTANT NOTE:

1) All plans are drawn to conform to one or more of the building industry's major national building standards at the time and place they were drawn. However, due to the variety of local building regulations, your plan may need to be modified to comply with local requirements—snow loads, energy loads, seismic zones, etc. We strongly recommend that you consult with your local building officials or local architect for required information on submission of permit documents.

2) Detail plans are generic and do not conform specifically to the house plan that you purchase.

*Multiple sets of documents (blueprints) may be required by your local village or municipality building depts.

PRICE CODE*

	A	B	C	D	E	F
BLUEPRINTS (Material List subject to availability)						
One Set of Blueprints	$195.00	$230.00	$275.00	$320.00	$520.00	$720.00
Four Sets of Blueprints	$265.00	$310.00	$355.00	$400.00	$1,020.00	$1,220.00
Seven Sets of Blueprints	$320.00	$360.00	$405.00	$450.00	$1,420.00	$1,620.00
Reproducible Vellum (1 Set)	$480.00	$540.00	$600.00	$675.00	$1,645.00	$1,845.00
Reproducible Mylar (1 Set)	$500.00	$560.00	$620.00	$695.00	$1,665.00	$1,865.00
Additional regular sets	$40.00	$40.00	$40.00	$40.00	$180.00	$180.00
Mirror reverse	$40.00	$40.00	$40.00	$40.00	$180.00	$180.00
SHIPPING AND HANDLING 1–7 sets						
Regular U.S.(6-10 days)	$10.00	$13.00	$16.00	$19.00	$22.00	$25.00
Express (2-3 days)	$25.00	$28.00	$31.00	$34.00	$37.00	$40.00
Overnight*	$30.00	$33.00	$36.00	$39.00	$42.00	$45.00
Other**	Call	Call	Call	Call	Call	Call
*Not available on certain plans **For delivery outside U.S.						
MATERIAL LIST *Material list subject to availability						
1-3 copies	$40.00	$40.00	$40.00	$40.00	CALL	CALL
4-7 copies	$45.00	$45.00	$45.00	$45.00	CALL	CALL
PREVIEW PLANS (11" X 17" format)						
1 ea. B/W format*	$15.00	$15.00	$15.00	$15.00	CALL	CALL
1 ea. Colored format*	$40.00	$40.00	$40.00	$40.00	CALL	CALL
*Subject to availability						
1 ea. B/W sell sheets*	$25.00	$25.00	$25.00	$25.00	—	—
100 qty. ea. B/W sell sheets*	$38.00	$38.00	$38.00	$38.00	—	—
200 qty. ea. B/W sell sheets*	$58.00	$58.00	$58.00	$58.00	—	—
ARCHITECTURAL RENDERING OF HOME B/W 8"X10" PMT Format*	$89.00	$89.00	$89.00	$89.00	CALL	CALL
Colored 8"X10" PMT format*	$115.00	$115.00	$115.00	$115.00	CALL	CALL

*Subject to availability

BLUEPRINTS ORDER FORM

Step 1.

PURCHASED BOOK FROM: _____ TOWN: _____

DATE BOOK WAS PURCHASED: _____

NAME: _____

ADDRESS: _____

CITY: _____ STATE: _____ ZIP: _____

PHONE #: ( ) _____

Enclosed is: ☐ Check   ☐ Money Order

Bill: ☐ Visa   ☐ Master Card

Checks Payable to: NPS Design America, Inc.

Step 3.

CARD NUMBER: _____

EXPIRATION DATE MONTH/YEAR_____/_____

SIGNATURE

Detail Plans

_____ **H801C Construction**
@ $14.95 each

_____ **H802E Electrical**
@ $14.95 each

_____ **H803P Plumbing**
@ $14.95 each

Any two (2) - $22.96

Any three (3) - $29.97

Write in dollar figure

$_____ Detail plans

$_____ Blueprints

$_____ Material List

$_____ Preview Plans

$_____ Design Sheets

$_____ Arch Rendering

$_____ Shipping & Handling

$_____ Sub Total

$_____ Sales Tax (IL 6.75%)

$_____ **Total**

Step 2.

Plan Number _____ Price Code_____

Foundation Type:_____
(Many plans offer different options; others are designed to one type of condition).

Number of Sets: ____One Set   ____Four Sets   ____Seven Sets   ____Vellum   ____Mylar

Additional Sets: _____ Qty. ($40.00 Price Code A-D; Price Code E-F Call) Prices good for 60 days

Mirror Reverse:_____ ($40.00)

Material List: _____(See List)

Preview Plan Number: _____ (See List)

Design Sheets: ____1ea. ____100 qty. ____200 qty. of Plan Number:_____
(Check appropriate space)

Architectural Rendering: _____B/W   _____Colored (See List) Plan Number:_____

Send Your Order To: NPS Design America, Inc.
Slot A-1 P.O. Box 66973 Dept. DA1000, Chicago, IL, 60666-0973

Order Toll Free 1-800-533-4350 Or 24-Hour Fax Ordering 1-800-344-4293

*Prices may change without notice

PLAN VL947

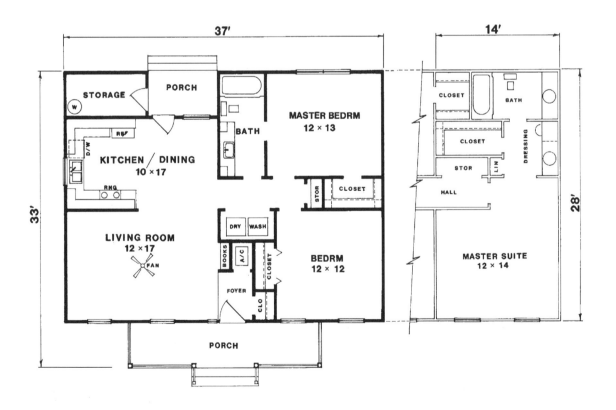

37'

STORAGE
W

PORCH

BATH

MASTER BEDRM
12 × 13

KITCHEN / DINING
10 × 17

RS

D/W

RNG

33'

LIVING ROOM
12 × 17
FAN

DRY WASH

BOOKS A/C

CLOSET

STOR CLOSET

BEDRM
12 × 12

FOYER

CLO

PORCH

14'

CLOSET BATH

CLOSET

STOR LIN

HALL

DRESSING

MASTER SUITE
12 × 14

28'

Total Living Area   **947 sq. ft.**

PRICE CODE: A

CUSTOMIZE IT!

ORDER TOLL FREE   **1 ▪ 800 ▪ 533 ▪ 4350**   24-HOUR FAX ORDERING   **1 ▪ 800 ▪ 344 ▪ 4293**

34

PLAN SH70-981

35

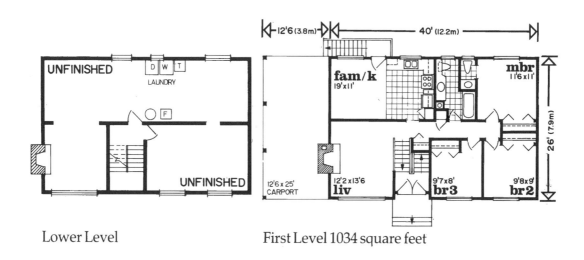

Lower Level

First Level 1034 square feet

Features

- Living room overlooks the cathedral entry.
- Country kitchen, with ample space for a breakfast table, flows to a family room.
- Master bedroom has a two-piece ensuite.

- Unfinished lower level provides 939 square feet for future development.
- Lower level may be used for additional bedrooms, den or in-law suite.

Total Living Area   **1,034 sq. ft.**

PRICE CODE: A

CUSTOMIZE IT!

ORDER TOLL FREE   1▪800▪533▪4350   **24-HOUR FAX ORDERING**   1▪800▪344▪4293

PLAN NPES111

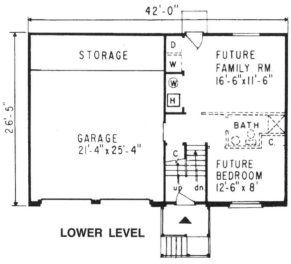

42'-0"

26'-5"

STORAGE

D
W
W
H

FUTURE
FAMILY RM.
16'-6"x11'-6"

GARAGE
21'-4" x 25'-4"

BATH

C.

C
up dn.

FUTURE
BEDROOM
12'-6" x 8'

LOWER LEVEL

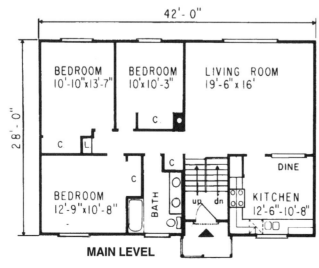

42'-0"

28'-0"

BEDROOM
10'-10"x13'-7"

BEDROOM
10'x10'-3"

LIVING ROOM
19'-6"x16'

C.

C

C

BEDROOM
12'-9"x10'-8"

C

BATH

C
up dn.

DINE

KITCHEN
12'-6"-10'-8"

MAIN LEVEL

36

Features

- This contemporary bi-level allows for future expansion as your family grows.
- Energy-saving designs feature three bedrooms clustered at left wing of main level.
- One full bath serves all bedrooms.
- Two-car garage is located on lower level.
- Truss roof construction allows adjustment for different roof loads.

Main level	**1,164 sq. ft.**
Lower Level	**534 sq. ft.**
Total Living Area	**1,698 sq. ft.**

PRICE CODE: B

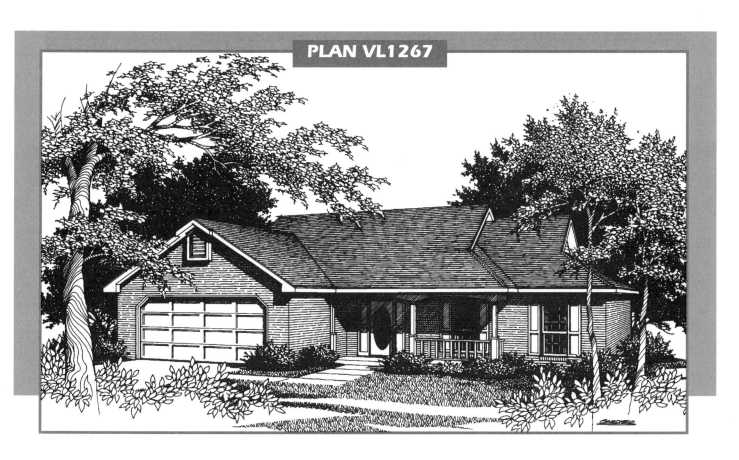

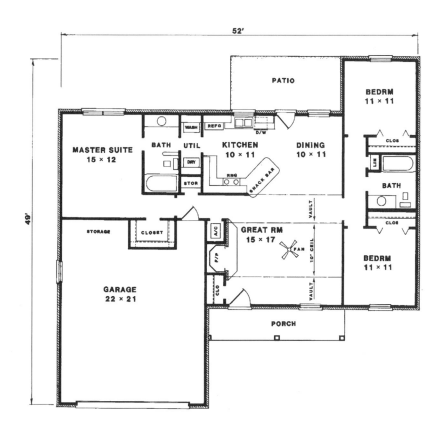

Total Living Area   1,267 sq. ft.

PRICE CODE: A

PLAN SH95-1282

38

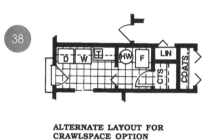

**ALTERNATE LAYOUT FOR
CRAWLSPACE OPTION**

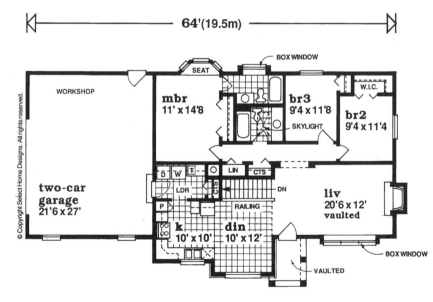

64' (19.5m)

34' (10.4m)

BOX WINDOW
SEAT
WORKSHOP
mbr
11' x 14'8
br3
9'4 x 11'8
W.I.C.
br2
9'4 x 11'4
SKYLIGHT
two-car
garage
21'6 x 27'
LIN
CTS
LDR
CTS
DN
RAILING
liv
20'6 x 12'
vaulted
P
k
10' x 10'
din
10' x 12'
VAULTED
BOX WINDOW

FLOOR PLAN 1282 sq.ft.

Features

- Intricate exterior detailing of porch gables and fish-scale siding bring back memories of yesterday.
- Main living areas are situated to enjoy a front view with the bedrooms privately set to the rear of the home.
- Master bedroom is complete with a bay window, sufficient closet and a full three-piece ensuite.

- Extra-large garage is ideal for all types of workplan shop activities.
- Future development can be made in unfinished basement.

Total Living Area: 1,282 sq. ft.

PRICE CODE: A

CUSTOMIZE IT!

ORDER TOLL FREE 1■800■533■4350 24-HOUR FAX ORDERING 1■800■344■4293

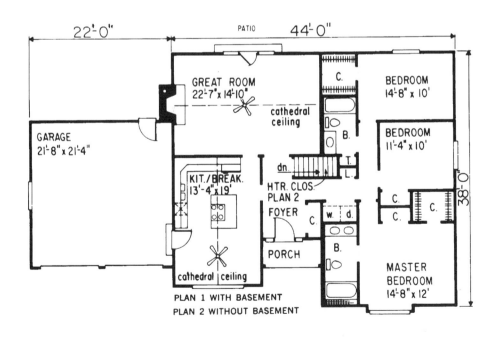

GARAGE
21'-8" x 21'-4"

GREAT ROOM
22'-7" x 14'-10"
cathedral ceiling

KIT./BREAK.
13'-4" x 19'
cathedral ceiling

HTR. CLOS.
PLAN 2

FOYER

PORCH

PATIO

22'-0" 44'-0"

C.

B.

dn.

T.
L.

w. d.

C.

B.

38'-0"

BEDROOM
14'-8" x 10'

BEDROOM
11'-4" x 10'

C. C.
C.

MASTER
BEDROOM
14'-8" x 12'

PLAN 1 WITH BASEMENT
PLAN 2 WITHOUT BASEMENT

Lighted Charm

Features

- Porch entrance into foyer leads to an impressive dining area with full window with half-circle window above.
- Kitchen/breakfast room features a center island and cathedral ceiling.
- Great room with cathedral ceiling and exposed beams accessible from foyer.
- Master bedroom includes full bath and walk-in closet.
- Two additional bedrooms share a full bath.

Total Living Area **1,540 sq. ft.**

PRICE CODE: B

CUSTOMIZE IT!

ORDER TOLL FREE 1∙800∙533∙4350   24-HOUR FAX ORDERING 1∙800∙344∙4293

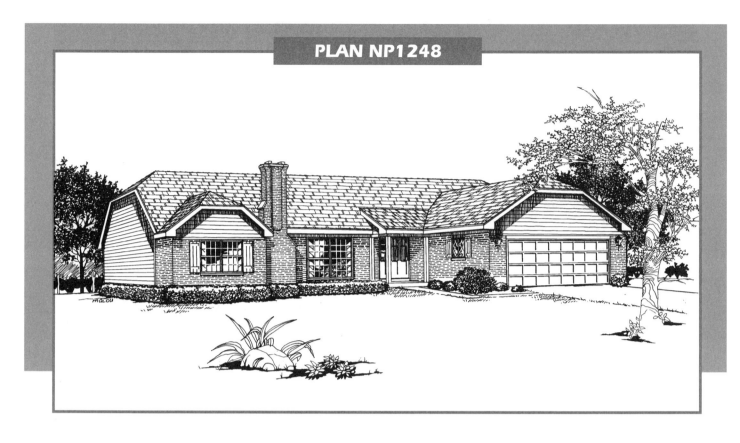

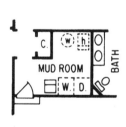

PLAN 2 WITHOUT BASEMENT

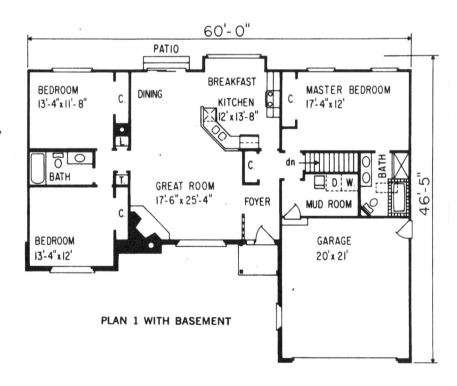

PLAN 1 WITH BASEMENT

Morning Glory

Features

- Distinctive one-story home with efficient floor plan.
- Foyer enters into open great room with corner fireplace and rear dining room with adjoining kitchen.
- Left wing includes two bedrooms with full bath.

- Right wing includes master bedroom with full bath.
- Garage access to home enters mud room/laundry.

Total Living Area   1,574 sq. ft.

PRICE CODE: B

PLAN FD8265-L

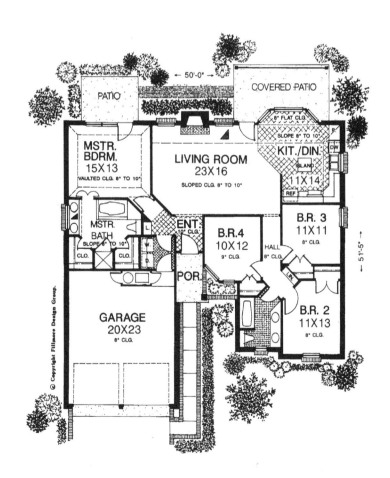

PATIO

COVERED PATIO

← 50'-0" →

MSTR. BDRM.
15X13
VAULTED CLG. 8' TO 10'

LIVING ROOM
23X16
SLOPED CLG. 8' TO 10'

8' FLAT CLG.
SLOPE 8' TO 10'

KIT./DIN.
11X14
ISLAND
REF

MSTR. BATH
SLOPE 8' TO 10'
CLO. CLO.

ENT.
10' CLG.

B.R. 4
10X12
9' CLG.

POR.

HALL
8' CLG.

B.R. 3
11X11
8' CLG.

51'-5"

B.R. 2
11X13
8' CLG.

GARAGE
20X23
8' CLG.

© Copyright Fillmore Design Group.

41

Total Living Area   1,584 sq. ft.

PRICE CODE: B

42

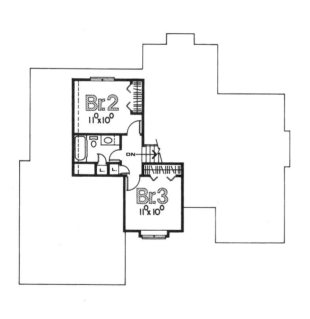

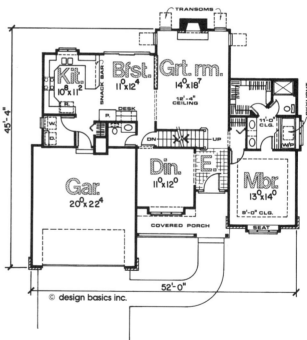

© design basics inc.

Features

- Welcoming covered porch.
- Entry views formal dining room with boxed window and great room beyond.
- Beautiful fireplace flanked by tall corner windows in volume great room.
- Powder bath conveniently located.
- Closet at garage entry.
- Window in laundry room.

- Open kitchen/dinette area features pantry, desk and snack bar counter.
- Elegant master suite with formal ceiling detail and window seat.
- Skylight above whirlpool, decorator plant shelf and double lavs in deluxe master dressing area.
- Secondary bedrooms share centrally located bathroom.

First Floor	1,297 sq. ft.
Second Floor	388 sq. ft.
Total Living Area	1,685 sq. ft.

PRICE CODE: C

PLAN DB3103

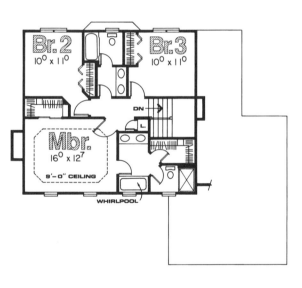

Br.2
10⁰ x 11⁰

Br.3
10⁰ x 11⁰

DN

Mbr.
16⁰ x 12⁷

9'-0" CEILING

WHIRLPOOL

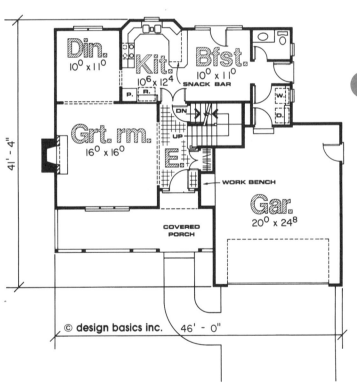

Din.
10⁰ x 11⁰

Kit.
10⁶ x 12⁴

Bfst.
10⁰ x 11⁰

SNACK BAR

P. R.

DN

UP

Grt. rm.
16⁰ x 16⁰

W. D.

WORK BENCH

Gar.
20⁰ x 24⁸

COVERED PORCH

41' - 4"

46' - 0"

© design basics inc.

43

Features

- Traditional elevation with covered porch provides mass appeal.
- U-stairs and French doors highlight entry.
- Large cased openings define formal dining room and great room without restricting space.
- Bayed kitchen and breakfast area have functional access to utility area and side yard.
- Secondary bedrooms share generous

compartmented bath with dual lavs.
- His and her walk-in closets, 9-foot-high boxed ceiling and whirlpool bath create stately master suite.
- Workbench and extra storage space in garage.

First Floor	904 sq. ft.
Second Floor	796 sq. ft.
Total Living Area	1,700 sq. ft.

PRICE CODE: C

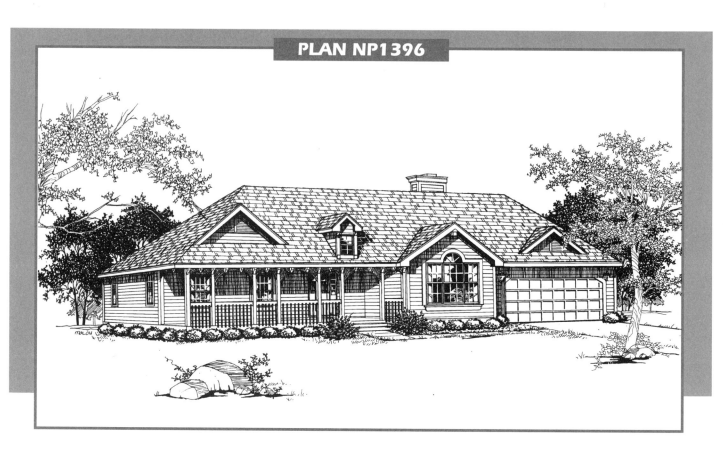

PLAN 2 WITHOUT BASEMENT

44

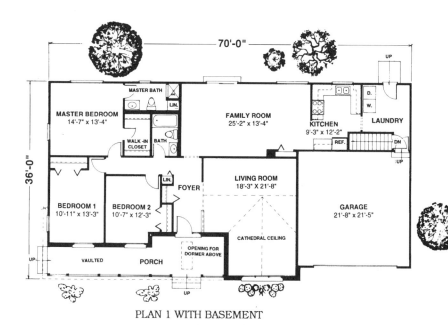

PLAN 1 WITH BASEMENT

Sunny Bower

Features

- Stunning design elements on exterior of this home make it a stand-out.
- Vaulted roof on wide front porch and unique porch dormer greet the eye.
- Porch entrance leads to ample foyer with entry closet.
- Step-down leads to large, cathedral-ceiling living room on the right.
- The left wing contains the master bedroom with master bath and walk-in closet.
- Two additional bedrooms share a full bath.

Total Living Area   1,820 sq. ft.

PRICE CODE: B

CUSTOMIZE IT!

ORDER TOLL FREE   1•800•533•4350   24-HOUR FAX ORDERING   1•800•344•4293

PLAN FD7034

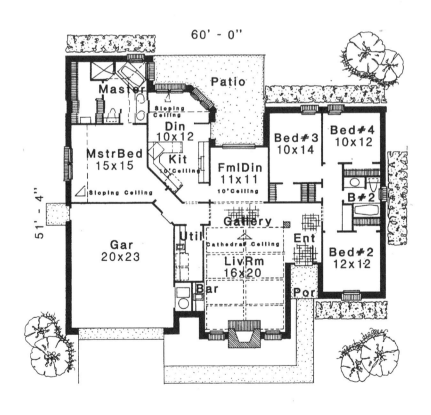

60' - 0"

51' - 4"

Master

Sloping Ceiling

Din 10x12

MstrBed 15x15

Kit 10'Ceiling

Sloping Ceiling

Patio

FmlDin 11x11 10'Ceiling

Bed#3 10x14

Bed#4 10x12

B#2

Gar 20x23

Util

Gallery

Cathedral Ceiling

LivRm 16x20

Bar

Ent

Por

Bed#2 12x12

Total Living Area   1,936 sq. ft.

PRICE CODE: B

CUSTOMIZE IT!

ORDER TOLL FREE   1■800■533■4350   24-HOUR FAX ORDERING   1■800■344■4293

46

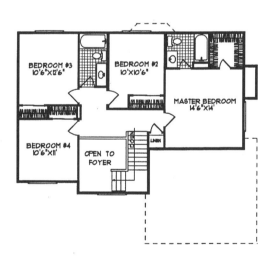

SECOND FLOOR PLAN

BEDROOM #3
10'6"x12'6"

BEDROOM #2
10'x10'6"

MASTER BEDROOM
14'6"x14'

BEDROOM #4
10'6"x11'

OPEN TO FOYER

LINEN

DOWN

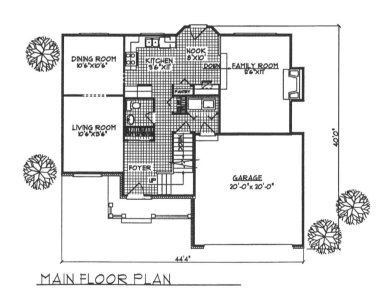

MAIN FLOOR PLAN

DINING ROOM
10'6"x10'6"

KITCHEN
9'6"x11'

NOOK
8'x10'

FAMILY ROOM
12'6"x17'

DOWN

PANTRY

LIVING ROOM
10'6"x13'6"

FOYER

UP

GARAGE
20'-0" x 20'-0"

44'4"

40'0"

First Floor	992 sq. ft.
Second Floor	950 sq. ft.
Total Living Area	1,942 sq. ft.

PRICE CODE: B

CUSTOMIZE IT!

ORDER TOLL FREE   1 ∎ 800 ∎ 533 ∎ 4350   24-HOUR FAX ORDERING   1 ∎ 800 ∎ 344 ∎ 4293

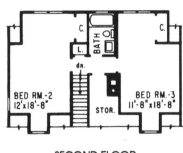

SECOND FLOOR

47

Colonial Fair

Features

- Colonial grace with practical application.
- Secluded master bedroom suite offers full bath and walk-in closet on first floor.
- Formal dining room and kitchen with informal dining area adjacent to spacious family room.
- Long living room features fireplace on interior wall.
- Service entry into the kitchen eliminates messy traffic from main entry.
- Two large upstairs bedrooms with full bath perfect for children.

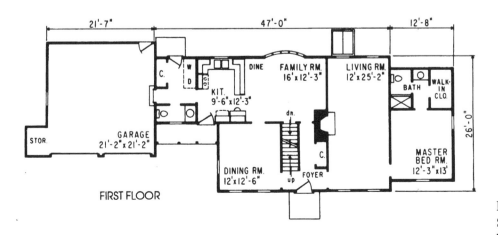

FIRST FLOOR

First Floor	1,337 sq. ft.
Second Floor	636 sq. ft.
Total Living Area	1,973 sq. ft.

PRICE CODE: B

PLAN FD7110

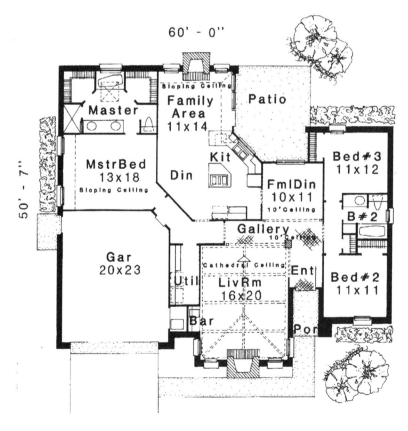

60' - 0''

50' - 7''

Master

Family Area
11x14

Patio

MstrBed
13x18
Sloping Ceiling

Kit

Din

Bed#3
11x12

FmlDin
10x11
10' Ceiling

B#2

Gar
20x23

Gallery
10' Ceiling

Util

Cathedral Ceiling

Bed#2
11x11

LivRm
16x20

Ent

Bar

Por

Total Living Area   1,980 sq. ft.

PRICE CODE: B

48

49

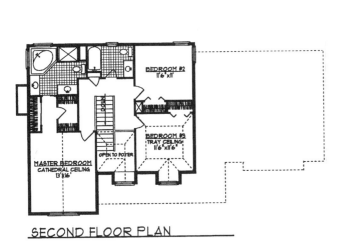

SECOND FLOOR PLAN

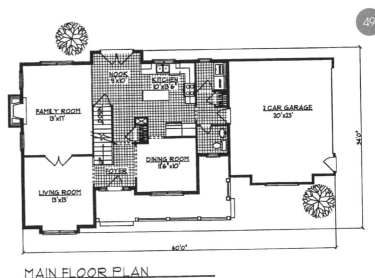

MAIN FLOOR PLAN

First Floor	1,065 sq. ft.
Second Floor	921 sq. ft.
Total Living Area	1,986 sq. ft.

PRICE CODE: B

CUSTOMIZE IT!

ORDER TOLL FREE   1▪800▪533▪4350   24-HOUR FAX ORDERING   1▪800▪344▪4293

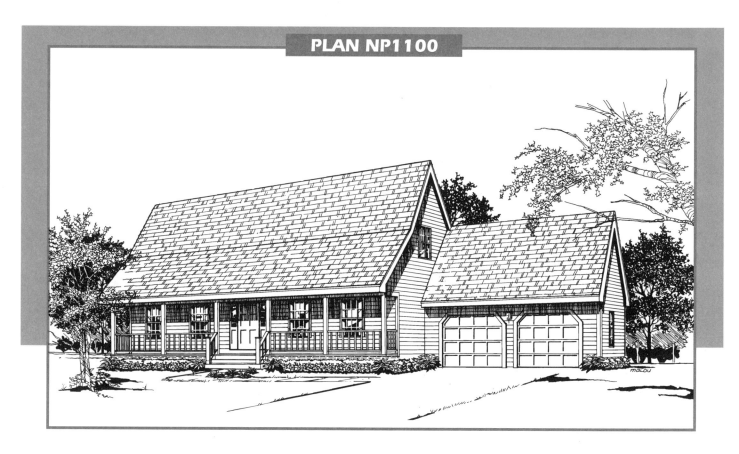

SECOND FLOOR

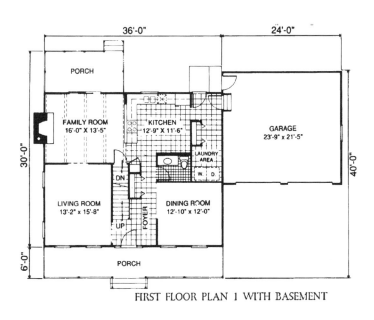

FIRST FLOOR PLAN 1 WITH BASEMENT

Down-Home Delight

Features

- Nothing could be sweeter than to view this home as yours.
- Beautiful, front-spanning porch exudes warmth.
- Living room and dining room flank the entrance hall.
- Cozy family room features beamed ceiling and fireplace.
- L-shaped kitchen roomy enough for small dining table.
- Upstairs, master bedroom has generous walk-in closet and private bath.
- Two additional upstairs bedrooms are served by full bath.

First Floor	1,080 sq. ft.
Second Floor	868 sq. ft.
Total Living Area	1,948 sq. ft.

PRICE CODE: B

PLAN SH77-1909

Total Living Area: 2,020 sq. ft.

51

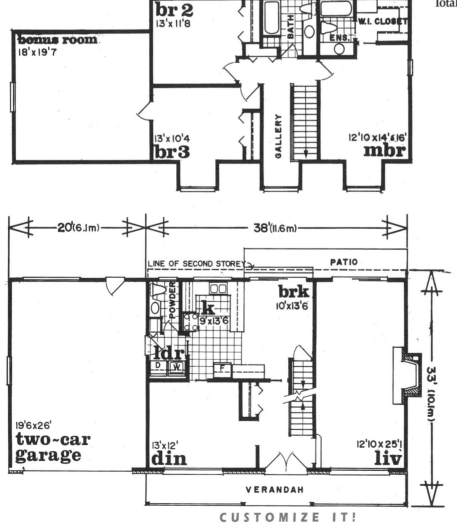

bonus room
18'x19'7

br 2
13'x11'8

BATH

W.I. CLOSET

ENS.

br 3
13'x10'4

GALLERY

mbr
12'10 x14'&16'

20'(6.1m)

38'(11.6m)

LINE OF SECOND STOREY

PATIO

POWDER

brk
10'x13'6

k
9'x13'6

ldr
D W

F

33' (10.1m)

two-car garage
19'6x26'

din
13'x12'

liv
12'10 x25'1

VERANDAH

Features

- Inviting country home is enhanced by full-width covered front porch, fieldstone exterior and a trio of dormers.
- Large sunken living room has feature fireplace.
- Living room extends from the front to the rear of the house.
- U-shaped kitchen adjoins the breakfast room.
- Garage access is a few short steps from the kitchen through the laundry room.
- Sliding glass doors from the rear patio open to the breakfast area and living room.
- Master bedroom features a dormer alcove and walk-in closet. Spacious bonus room provides an additional 377 square feet of living space.

PRICE CODE: B

PLAN SH91-2056

52

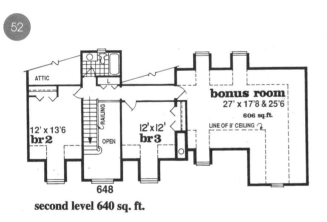

ATTIC

12' x 13'6
br 2

RAILING
OPEN

12' x 12'
br 3

648

bonus room
27' x 17'8 & 25'6
606 sq.ft.

LINE OF 8' CEILING

second level 640 sq. ft.

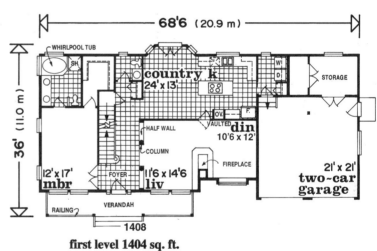

68'6 (20.9 m)

WHIRLPOOL TUB

SH

36' (11.0 m)

country k
24' x 13'

STORAGE

W
D

OV
F.

VAULTED

din
10'6 x 12'

HALF WALL

COLUMN

12' x 17'
mbr

FOYER

11'6 x 14'6
liv

FIREPLACE

21' x 21'
two~car
garage

RAILING

VERANDAH

1408

first level 1404 sq. ft.

Features

- Two-storey foyer is flanked by the master bedroom and living room.
- Open living and dining room is divided by a three-way fireplace.
- Country kitchen hosts a centre cooking island and is conveniently located to the laundry area.
- Two-car garage has space for extra storage

or a workplan shop.
- Master bedroom ensuite boasts a whirlpool tub in a sunlit corner, double vanity, separate plan shower and spacious walk-in closet.

Total Living Area: 2,044 sq. ft.

PRICE CODE: B

CUSTOMIZE IT!

ORDER TOLL FREE 1■800■533■4350   24-HOUR FAX ORDERING 1■800■344■4293

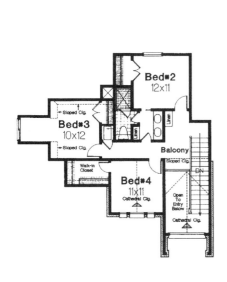

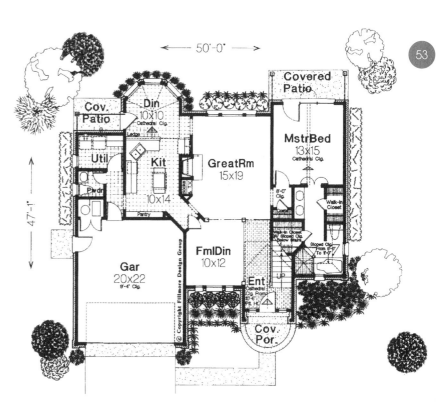

First Floor	1,359 sq. ft.
Second Floor	697 sq. ft.
Total Living Area	2,056 sq. ft.

PRICE CODE: B

PLAN FD8166-L

Total Living Area   2,061 sq. ft.

PRICE CODE: B

55

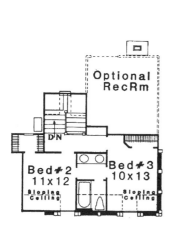

Optional RecRm

DN

Bed #2 11x12
Sloping Ceiling

Bed #3 10x13
Sloping Ceiling

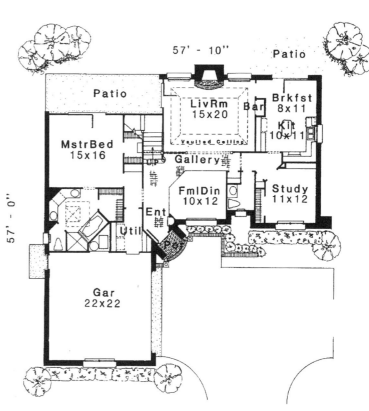

57' - 10"

Patio

Patio

LivRm 15x20
Vaulted Ceiling

Bar

Brkfst 8x11

Kit 10x11

MstrBed 15x16

57' - 0"

Gallery

FmlDin 10x12

Study 11x12

Ent

Util

Gar 22x22

First Floor	1,643 sq. ft.
Second Floor	422 sq. ft.
Total Living Area	2,065 sq. ft.

PRICE CODE: B

PLAN VL2069

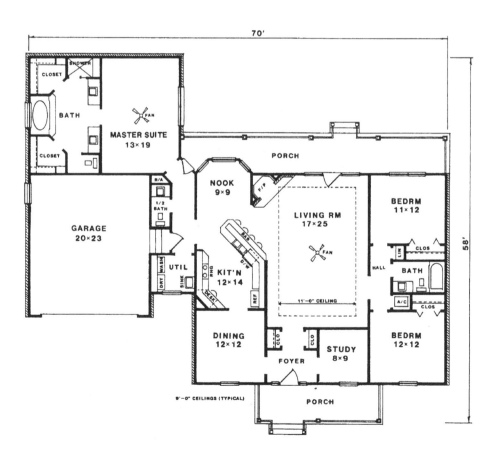

Total Living Area   **2,069 sq. ft.**

PRICE CODE: B

CUSTOMIZE IT!

ORDER TOLL FREE   1■800■533■4350   24-HOUR FAX ORDERING   1■800■344■4293

PLAN FD8162-L

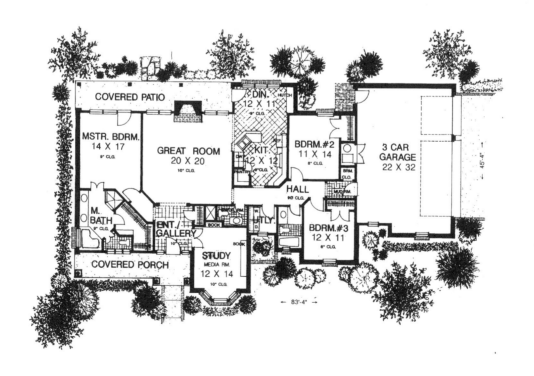

COVERED PATIO

DIN.
12 X 11

MSTR. BDRM.
14 X 17
9' CLG.

GREAT ROOM
20 X 20
10' CLG.

KIT.
12 X 12

BDRM.#2
11 X 14
8' CLG.

3 CAR GARAGE
22 X 32

45'-4"

HALL

M. BATH

ENT./GALLERY

UTLY.

BDRM.#3
12 X 11
8' CLG.

COVERED PORCH

STUDY
MEDIA RM.
12 X 14
10' CLG.

83'-4"

Total Living Area   2,086 sq. ft.

PRICE CODE: B

PLAN SH1189-2073

58

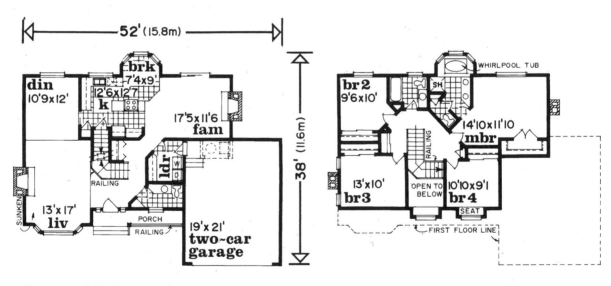

First Level 1062 square feet

Second Level 1026 square feet

Features

- Dormer window brightens foyer and open staircase.
- Sunken living room boasts bay window and masonry fireplace.
- Kitchen, with centre cooking island, is open to breakfast bay and family room.

- Family room has masonry fireplace and sliding glass walk-through to patio.
- Master bedroom features walk-in closet and lavish ensuite.
- Ensuite features spa, tucked in windowed-bay, twin vanity and shower.

Total Living Area   **2,088 sq. ft.**

PRICE CODE: B

CUSTOMIZE IT!

ORDER TOLL FREE   1▪800▪533▪4350   24-HOUR FAX ORDERING   1▪800▪344▪4293

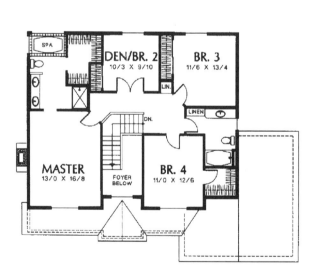

SPA

DEN/BR. 2
10/3 X 9/10

BR. 3
11/6 X 13/4

LIN.

LINEN

DN.

MASTER
13/0 X 16/8

FOYER BELOW

BR. 4
11/0 X 12/6

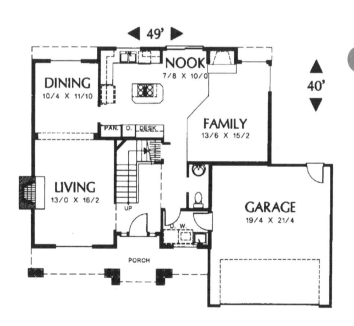

◀ 49' ▶

▲
40'
▼

59

DINING
10/4 X 11/10

NOOK
7/8 X 10/0

FAMILY
13/6 X 15/2

PAN. O. DESK

LIVING
13/0 X 16/2

UP

GARAGE
19/4 X 21/4

D. W.

PORCH

First Floor	1,032 sq. ft.
Second Floor	1,075 sq. ft.
Total Living Area	2,107 sq. ft.

PRICE CODE: B

PLAN FD7294

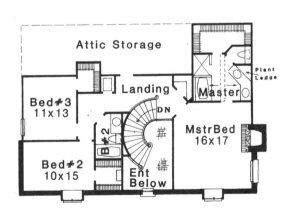

Upper Floor

Attic Storage

Bed #3
11x13

Landing

Master

Plant
Ledge

Bed #2
10x15

B #2

DN

MstrBed
16x17

Ent
Below

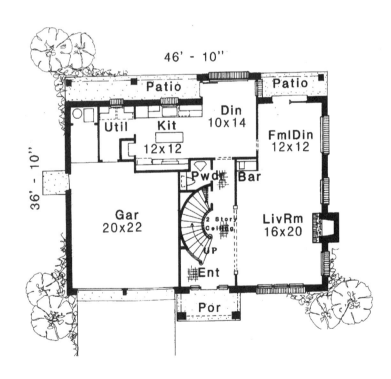

46' - 10''

36' - 10''

Patio

Patio

Din
10x14

Util

Kit
12x12

FmlDin
12x12

Pwdr

Bar

Gar
20x22

2 Story
Ceiling

LivRm
16x20

Ent

UP

Por

First Floor	1,085 sq. ft.
Second Floor	1,023 sq. ft.
Total Living Area	2,108 sq. ft.

PRICE CODE: B

CUSTOMIZE IT!

ORDER TOLL FREE 1▪800▪533▪4350   24-HOUR FAX ORDERING 1▪800▪344▪4293

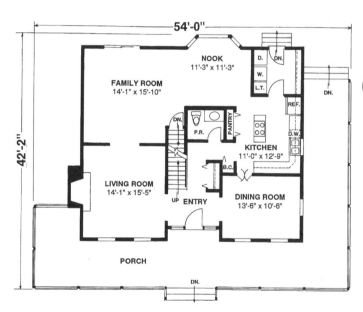

61

Stately Country

Features

- Combine country comfort with stately simplicity in this home.
- Wide, wrap-around porch brackets the front and right side of this home.
- At the left, a large living room with fireplace leads to a family room and bay-windowed nook.

- At right, a dining room is accessed from the large kitchen with centrally located cooking island and built-in pantry by swinging, saloon-style doors.
- Upstairs, master bedroom includes a dressing area with roof window, walk-in closet, and full bath.

First Floor	1,216 sq. ft.
Second Floor	896 sq. ft.
Total Living Area	2,112 sq. ft.

PRICE CODE: B

PLAN DB2285

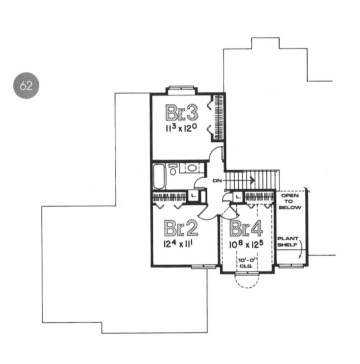

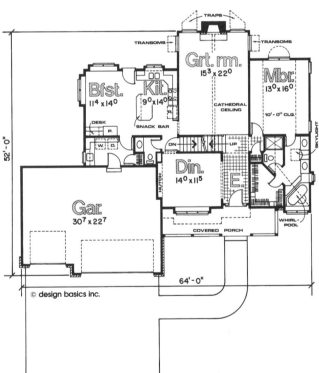

© design basics inc.

Features

- Expansive front elevation enhanced by covered porch alludes to sophisticated interior.
- Dramatic entry surveys dining room with hutch space and elegant great room beyond.
- Expansiveness of great room is enriched by cathedral ceiling and trapezoid windows.
- Kitchen/breakfast area with nearby laundry and powder bath is designed for convenience and ease of living.
- Secondary bedrooms secluded on second level, bedroom #4 with volume ceiling and \arched window.
- Main floor master suite contains skylit dressing area, corner whirlpool and spacious walk-in closet.

First Floor	1,505 sq. ft.
Second Floor	610 sq. ft.
Total Living Area	2,115 sq. ft.

PRICE CODE: C

PLAN FD8028A

63

Total Living Area   2,118 sq. ft.

PRICE CODE: B

PLAN DB826

OPTIONAL
WHIRLPOOL
BATH

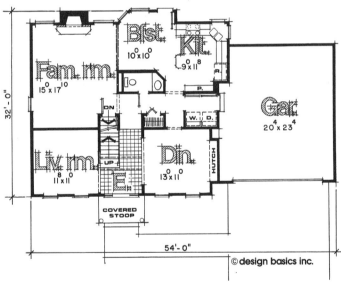

© design basics inc.

Features

- Dining room with hutch space and views to the outside through charming double-hung windows.
- Handsome wood railing separates large family room with fireplace from breakfast area.
- Efficient kitchen includes corner sink, pantry, island counter and breakfast area with access to the outside.
- Coat closet convenient to main and service entries.
- Master suite includes vaulted ceiling, 2 walk-in closets and double vanity.
- Third and fourth bedrooms offer private walk-in closets.
- Secondary bedrooms share central hall bath with 10-foot ceiling.

First Floor	**1,038 sq. ft.**
Second Floor	**1,080 sq. ft.**
Total Living Area	**2,118 sq. ft.**

PRICE CODE: C

CUSTOMIZE IT!

ORDER TOLL FREE 1■800■533■4350   **24-HOUR FAX ORDERING**   1■800■344■4293

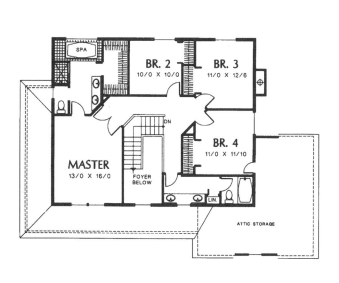

BR. 2
10/0 X 10/0

BR. 3
11/0 X 12/6

SPA

MASTER
13/0 X 16/0

BR. 4
11/0 X 11/10

FOYER
BELOW

DN

LIN.

ATTIC STORAGE

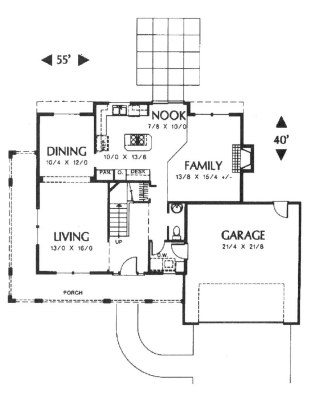

◄ 55' ►

▲
40'
▼

NOOK
7/8 X 10/0

DINING
10/4 X 12/0

10/0 X 13/8

FAMILY
13/8 X 15/4 +/-

REF.

PAN. O. DESK

LIVING
13/0 X 16/0

UP

D.W.

GARAGE
21/4 X 21/8

PORCH

First Floor	1,037 sq. ft.
Second Floor	1,090 sq. ft.
Total Living Area	2,127 sq. ft.

PRICE CODE: B

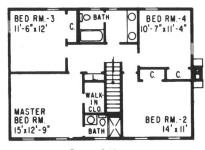

Second Floor

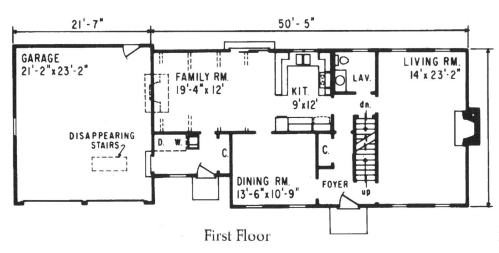

First Floor

Bryrewood Deluxe

Features

- Graciousness and convenient living are the themes of this Early American home.
- Designed for a family with children.
- Entry hall leads to U-shaped kitchen.
- Long, exposed beam family room with optional fireplace includes access to backyard.
- Living room with fireplace occupies the right side of the home.
- Second-floor master bedroom includes private bath and walk-in closet.
- Three additional bedrooms upstairs share a large bath with double-vanity.
- Garage loft, reached by disappearing stairs, adds extra space for hobby or play room

First Floor	1,149 sq. ft.
Second Floor	988 sq. ft.
Total Living Area	2,137 sq. ft.

PRICE CODE: B

PLAN AM2265B

◀ 54' ▶

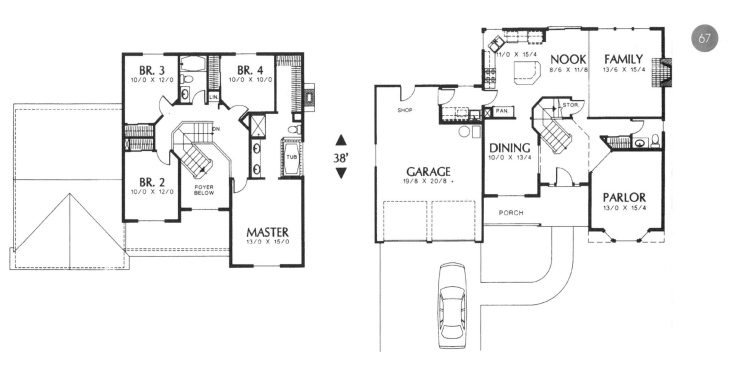

38'

67

First Floor	1,157 sq. ft.
Second Floor	980 sq. ft.
Total Living Area	2,137 sq. ft.

PRICE CODE: B

PLAN NP1112

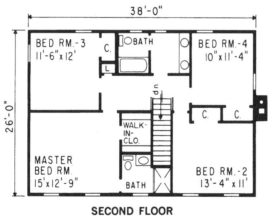

38'-0"

26'-0"

BED RM.-3
11'-6" x 12'

BATH

C.

BED RM.-4
10" x 11'-4"

L

WALK-
IN-
CLO.

up

C.

C.

MASTER
BED RM.
15' x 12'-9"

BATH

BED RM.-2
13'-4" x 11'

SECOND FLOOR

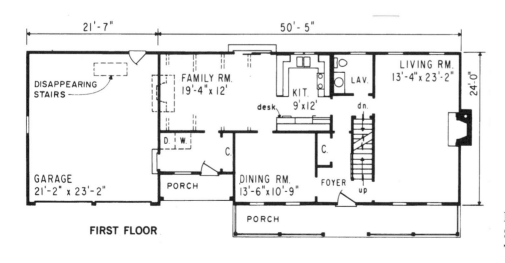

21'-7"

50'-5"

24'-0"

DISAPPEARING
STAIRS

FAMILY RM.
19'-4" x 12'

KIT.
9' x 12'

desk

LAV.

LIVING RM.
13'-4" x 23'-2"

dn.

D. | W.

C.

GARAGE
21'-2" x 23'-2"

PORCH

DINING RM.
13'-6" x 10'-9"

C.

FOYER

up

dn.

PORCH

FIRST FLOOR

Colonial Silhouette

Features

- Wide front porch spans the front of this beautiful colonial home.
- Foyer opens to living room with fireplace on the right and formal dining room on the left.
- Second, porch-covered entrance leads to the mud room and family room with exposed beam ceiling.
- First-floor lavatory.
- Second floor includes three bed rooms and a full bath and a master bedroom with walk-in closet and private bath.
- Disappearing, pull-down stairs in garage to access storage space above

First Floor	1,149 sq. ft.
Second Floor	988 sq. ft.
Total Living Area	2,137 sq. ft.

PRICE CODE: B

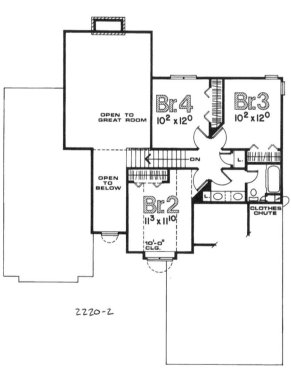

2220-2

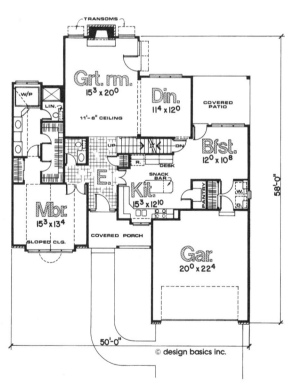

© design basics inc.

69

Features

- Arched window is seen in volume entry.
- Volume great room with handsome fireplace and windows out the back.
- Service doors to close off kitchen.
- Dining room and dinette both feature large windows out the back.
- Gourmet kitchen includes snack bar on island counter, desk and walk-in pantry.

- Convenient family entrance through laundry with closet.
- Beautiful arched window, double doors and sloped ceiling in master suite.
- Master dressing area includes 2-person whirlpool, his and her vanities.
- Compartmented hall bath serves secondary bedrooms.

First Floor	1,506 sq. ft.
Second Floor	633 sq. ft.
Total Living Area	2,139 sq. ft.

PRICE CODE: C

CUSTOMIZE IT!

PLAN FD7663-LA

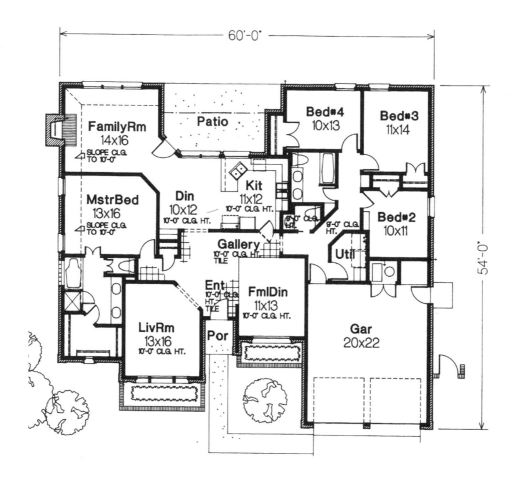

60'-0"

54'-0"

FamilyRm
14x16
SLOPE CLG.
TO 10'-0"

Patio

Bed#4
10x13

Bed#3
11x14

MstrBed
13x16
SLOPE CLG.
TO 10'-0"

Din
10x12
10'-0" CLG. HT.

Kit
11x12
10'-0" CLG. HT.

Bed#2
10x11

Gallery
10'-0" TILE

Ent
10'-0" CLG.
HT.
TILE

FmlDin
11x13
10'-0" CLG. HT.

Uti

LivRm
13x16
10'-0" CLG. HT.

Por

Gar
20x22

Total Living Area   2,140 sq. ft.

PRICE CODE: B

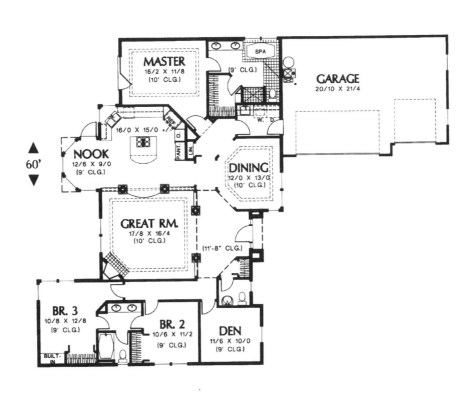

MASTER
16/2 X 11/8
(10' CLG.)

SPA
(9' CLG.)

GARAGE
20/10 X 21/4

W. D.

16/0 X 15/0

REF.

PANT. O.

LIN.

60'

NOOK
12/6 X 9/0
(9' CLG.)

DINING
12/0 X 13/0
(10' CLG.)

GREAT RM.
17/8 X 16/4
(10' CLG.)

(11'-8" CLG.)

BR. 3
10/8 X 12/8
(9' CLG.)

BR. 2
10/6 X 11/2
(9' CLG.)

DEN
11/6 X 10/0
(9' CLG.)

BUILT-IN

71

Total Living Area   **2,155 sq. ft.**

PRICE CODE: B

PLAN VL2162

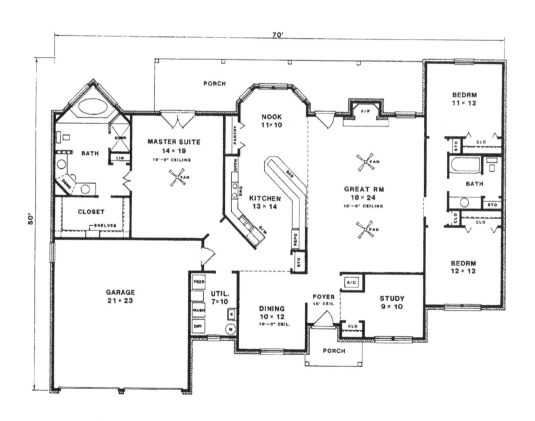

Total Living Area   2,162 sq. ft.

PRICE CODE: B

PLAN FD8074-LB

← 60'-0" →

54'-4"

Covered Patio

MstrBed 13x16
Slope Clg. To 11'-0"
Slope Clg. To 10'-0"
Walk-in Closet

Din 11x11 9'-0" Clg. Ht.
Pantry

FamilyRm 14x18 9'-0" Clg. Ht.

Kit 11x14 9'-0" Clg. Ht.

Gallery 10'-0" Clg. Ht.

Ent 10'-0" Clg. Ht.

FmlDin 10x13 10'-0" Clg. HT.

LivRm 13x14 10'-0" Clg. HT.

Bed#4 10x12 8'-0" Clg. Ht.

Bed#3 11x13 8'-0" Clg. Ht.

Util 9'-0" Clg. Ht.

Pwdr

Bed#2 10x11 8'-0" Clg. Ht.

Gar 20x20 8'-4" Clg. Ht.

Total Living Area   **2,178 sq. ft.**

PRICE CODE: B

PLAN FD8074-LA

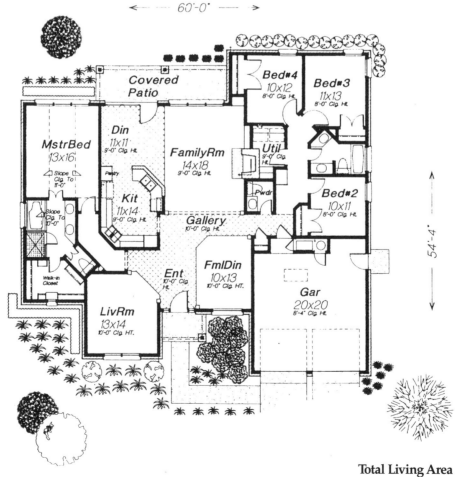

60'-0"

54'-4"

Covered Patio

MstrBed
13x16
Slope Clg. To 11'-0"
Slope Clg. To 10'-0"
Walk-in Closet

Din
11x11
9'-0" Clg. Ht.

Pantry

Kit
11x14
9'-0" Clg. Ht.

FamilyRm
14x18
9'-0" Clg. Ht.

Util
9'-0" Clg. Ht.

Pwdr

Gallery
10'-0" Clg. Ht.

Ent
10'-0" Clg. Ht.

FmlDin
10x13
10'-0" Clg. HT.

LivRm
13x14
10'-0" Clg. HT.

Bed#4
10x12
8'-0" Clg. Ht.

Bed#3
11x13
8'-0" Clg. Ht.

Bed#2
10x11
8'-0" Clg. Ht.

Gar
20x20
8'-4" Clg. Ht.

| Total Living Area | 2,178 sq. ft. |

PRICE CODE: B

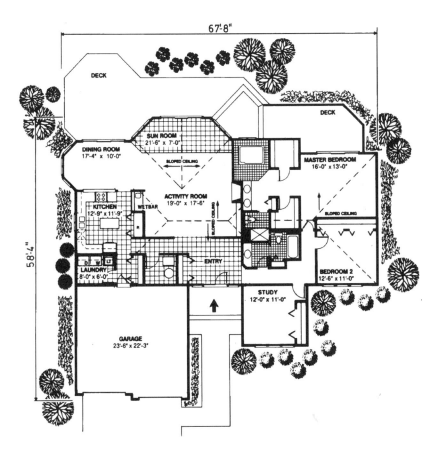

Sunny Retreat

Features

- Pleasing roof line angles and well-windowed entry catch the eye in this one-story home.
- Large, cathedral-ceiling entry leads to sloped ceiling activity room, sunken sun room.
- Wet bar in activity room is open to kitchen, which features a snack bar and serve-through to dining room.
- Garage entrance to home leads to laundry room and lavatory.
- Right wing of home includes a master bedroom with dual, walk-in closets, raised Roman tub and compartmented shower.
- Second bedroom with access to full bath.
- Front-facing study with closet would make a perfect office.

Total Living Area   **2,180 sq. ft.**

PRICE CODE: B

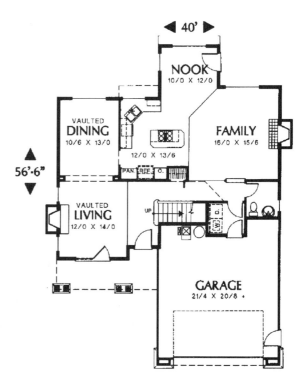

First Floor	1,110 sq. ft.
Second Floor	1,080 sq. ft.
Total Living Area	2,190 sq. ft.

PRICE CODE: B

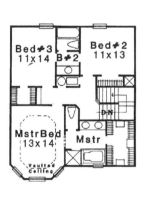

Bed #3
11x14

B #2

Bed #2
11x13

MstrBed
13x14
Vaulted Ceiling

Mstr

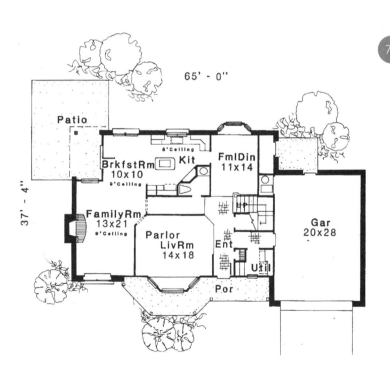

65' - 0"

37' - 4"

Patio

BrkfstRm
10x10
8'Ceiling

Kit

FmlDin
11x14

FamilyRm
13x21
8'Ceiling

Parlor
LivRm
14x18

Ent

Util

Gar
20x28

Por

First Floor	1,338 sq. ft.
Second Floor	862 sq. ft.
Total Living Area	2,200 sq. ft.

PRICE CODE: C

PLAN NP1134

MASTER BEDROOM
14'-10" x 14'-5"
BATH
BATH
BEDROOM
15'-10" x 12'-6"
BEDROOM
11'-4" x 12'-6"

SECOND FLOOR THREE BEDROOMS

MASTER BEDROOM
12' x 16'-8"
BATH
BEDROOM
13' x 11'
BATH
BEDROOM
15'-6" x 10'-2"
BEDROOM
11'-8" x 10'-2"

SECOND FLOOR FOUR BEDROOMS

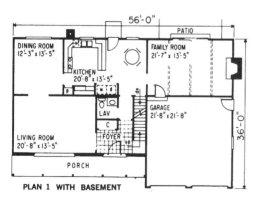

56'-0"
DINING ROOM
12'-3" x 13'-5"
KITCHEN
20'-8" x 13'-5"
PATIO
FAMILY ROOM
21'-7" x 13'-5"
LAV
GARAGE
21'-8" x 21'-8"
36'-0"
LIVING ROOM
20'-8" x 13'-5"
FOYER
PORCH

PLAN 1 WITH BASEMENT

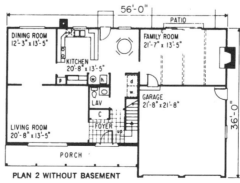

56'-0"
DINING ROOM
12'-3" x 13'-5"
KITCHEN
20'-8" x 13'-5"
PATIO
FAMILY ROOM
21'-7" x 13'-5"
LAV
GARAGE
21'-8" x 21'-8"
36'-0"
LIVING ROOM
20'-8" x 13'-5"
FOYER
PORCH

PLAN 2 WITHOUT BASEMENT

Classic Country

Features

- Enjoy the pleasures of front-porch sitting in this rustic-looking country home.
- Generously sized living room off foyer.
- Dining room adjacent to U-shaped kitchen with lunch counter and breakfast nook.
- Family room with beamed ceiling and fireplace.
- Second floor features a three- or four-bedroom option with two fulls baths.

First Floor	**1,260 sq. ft.**
Second Floor	**952 sq. ft.**
Total Living Area	**2,212 sq. ft.**

PRICE CODE: C

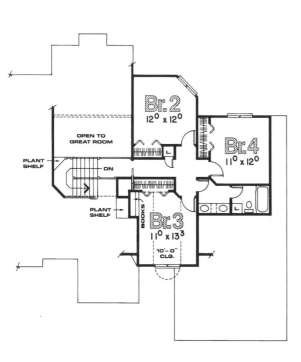

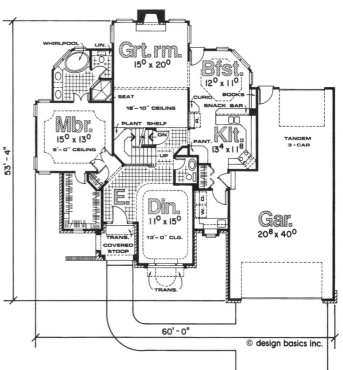

79

Features

- Formal roof lines and magnificent arched windows highlight front elevation.
- Flooring materials and special ceiling detail define dining room.
- Expansive great room features fireplace and is perfect for informal gatherings.
- Dramatic staircase overlooks secluded great room.
- Efficient kitchen features corner pantry and lazy Susan.
- French doors on angle lead to volume master suite.
- Double doors open to luxurious dressing area with large whirlpool and shower.
- Sloped ceiling, arched window and book shelves highlight bedroom #3.
- Tandem garage is ideal for boat or vintage car storage.

First Floor	1,518 sq. ft.
Second Floor	697 sq. ft.
Total Living Area	2,215 sq. ft.

PRICE CODE: C

80

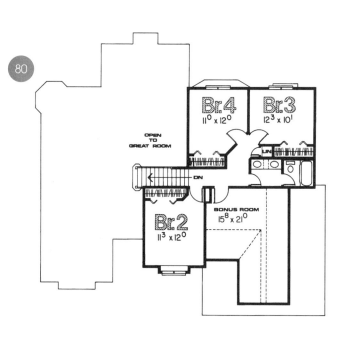

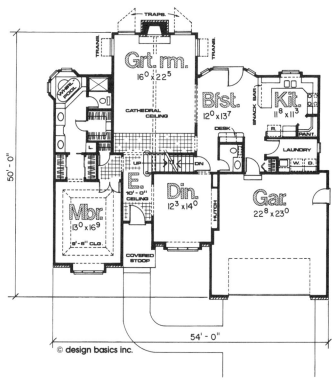

© design basics inc.

Features

- Boxed window and hutch space in formal dining room, snack bar, desk and walk-in pantry for kitchen.
- Bright open bayed dinette.
- Utility sink and window in laundry room.
- Conveniently located powder bath.

- Double doors into formal master suite.
- Dressing room with angled whirlpool, his and her vanities and 3 closets.
- Upstairs, bedrooms share compartmented bath with 2 lavs.

First Floor	1,593 sq. ft.
Second Floor	633 sq. ft.
Total Living Area	2,226 sq. ft.

PRICE CODE: D

PLAN FD8096-LB

Total Living Area   2,238 sq. ft.

PRICE CODE: C

CUSTOMIZE IT!

ORDER TOLL FREE   1 ▪ 800 ▪ 533 ▪ 4350   24-HOUR FAX ORDERING   1 ▪ 800 ▪ 344 ▪ 4293

PLAN FD8096-LA

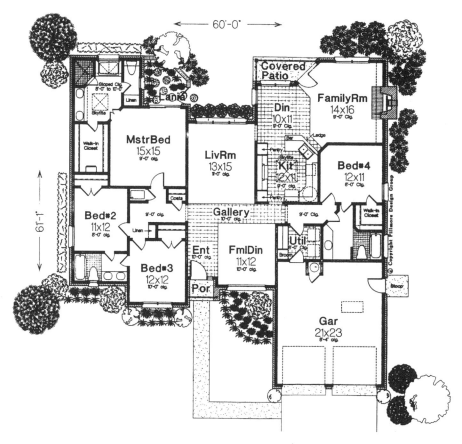

60'-0"

61'-1"

Covered Patio

FamilyRm
14x16
9'-0" Clg.

Din
10x11
9'-0" Clg.

MstrBed
15x15
9'-0" clg.

LivRm
13x15
11'-0" clg.

Kit
12x11
9'-0" Clg.

Bed#4
12x11
8'-0" Clg.

Walk-In Closet

Linen

Bed#2
11x12
8'-0" clg.

Gallery
10'-0" clg.

Walk-In Closet

Util
8'-0"

Ent
10'-0"

FmlDin
11x12
10'-0" clg.

Bed#3
12x12
10'-0" clg.

Por

Gar
21x23
8'-4" clg.

© Copyright Fillmore Design Group

Total Living Area 2,238 sq. ft.

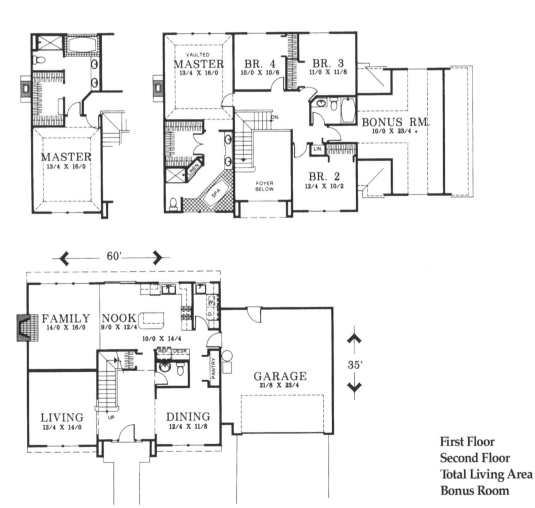

First Floor	1,167 sq. ft.
Second Floor	1,080 sq. ft.
Total Living Area	2,247 sq. ft.
Bonus Room	+358 sq. ft.

PRICE CODE: C

CUSTOMIZE IT!

ORDER TOLL FREE 1■800■533■4350   24-HOUR FAX ORDERING 1■800■344■4293

84

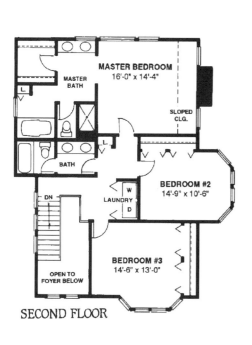

SECOND FLOOR

MASTER BEDROOM
16'-0" x 14'-4"

MASTER BATH

SLOPED CLG.

BATH

LAUNDRY

BEDROOM #2
14'-9" x 10'-6"

DN

BEDROOM #3
14'-6" x 13'-0"

OPEN TO FOYER BELOW

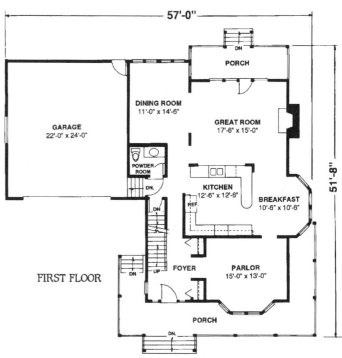

FIRST FLOOR

57'-0"

51'-8"

GARAGE
22'-0" x 24'-0"

DINING ROOM
11'-0" x 14'-6"

PORCH

GREAT ROOM
17'-6" x 15'-0"

POWDER ROOM

KITCHEN
12'-6" x 12'-6"

BREAKFAST
10'-6" x 10'-6"

REF.

DN

UP

FOYER

PARLOR
15'-0" x 13'-0"

PORCH

DN.

Victorian Hideaway

Features

- Contemporary comfort lodges in this compact Victorian design.
- Front parlor with bay window recaptures the charm of yesteryear.
- Centrally located kitchen shares counter with bay-windowed breakfast nook.

- Upstairs, the master bedroom, with dual-vanity bath, private water closet and shower area, and walk-in closet occupies the rear of the home.
- Two additional bedrooms share a deluxe bath.
- An upstairs laundry room adds to the convenience.

First Floor	1,203 sq. ft.
Second Floor	1,050 sq. ft.
Total Living Area	**2,253 sq. ft.**

PRICE CODE: C

CUSTOMIZE IT!

ORDER TOLL FREE 1■800■533■4350   24-HOUR FAX ORDERING 1■800■344■4293

58' - 3 CAR GARAGE
47' - 2 CAR GARAGE

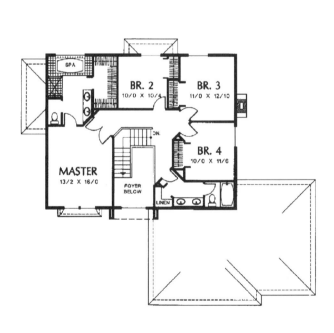

SPA

BR. 2
10/0 X 10/4

BR. 3
11/0 X 12/10

BR. 4
10/0 X 11/6

MASTER
13/2 X 16/0

FOYER BELOW

LINEN

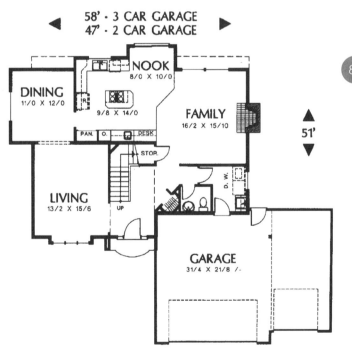

NOOK
8/0 X 10/0

DINING
11/0 X 12/0

9/8 X 14/0

FAMILY
16/2 X 15/10

51'

PAN. O.

DESK

STOR.

LIVING
13/2 X 15/6

UP

D. W.

GARAGE
31/4 X 21/8 /-

First Floor	1,180 sq. ft.
Second Floor	1,084 sq. ft.
Total Living Area	2,264 sq. ft.

PRICE CODE: C

CUSTOMIZE IT!

ORDER TOLL FREE   1 ∎ 800 ∎ 533 ∎ 4350   24-HOUR FAX ORDERING   1 ∎ 800 ∎ 344 ∎ 4293

PLAN FD6455-L

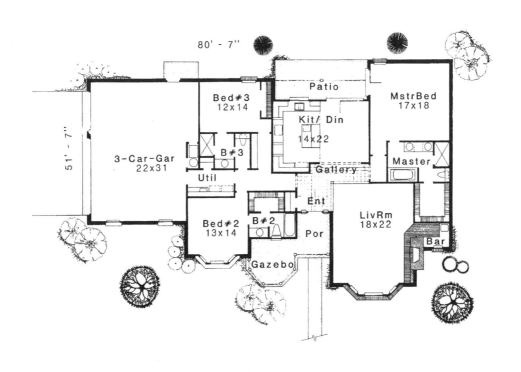

80' - 7''

51' - 7''

Bed #3
12x14

3-Car-Gar
22x31

B #3

Util

Patio

Kit/ Din
14x22

Gallery

MstrBed
17x18

Master

Bed #2
13x14

B #2

Ent

Por

LivRm
18x22

Bar

Gazebo

| Total Living Area | 2,267 sq. ft. |

PRICE CODE: C

CUSTOMIZE IT!

ORDER TOLL FREE 1■800■533■4350   24-HOUR FAX ORDERING 1■800■344■4293

PLAN SH91-2222

87

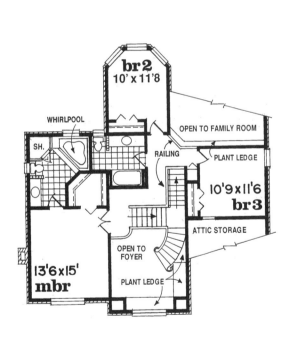

second level 969 sq. ft.

br2
10' x 11'8

WHIRLPOOL

SH.

OPEN TO FAMILY ROOM

RAILING

PLANT LEDGE

10'9 x 11'6
br3

ATTIC STORAGE

OPEN TO FOYER

13'6 x 15'
mbr

PLANT LEDGE

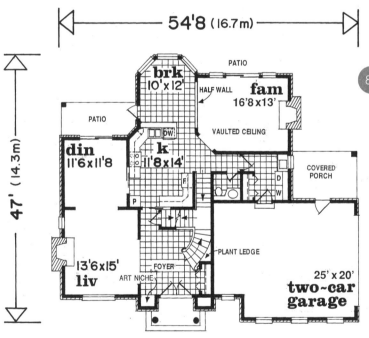

first level 1301 sq. ft.

54'8 (16.7 m)

47' (14.3 m)

PATIO

brk
10' x 12

HALF WALL

fam
16'8 x 13'

PATIO

VAULTED CEILING

din
11'6 x 11'8

k
11'8 x 14'

DW

F

COVERED PORCH

D W

PLANT LEDGE

13'6 x 15'
liv

ART NICHE

FOYER

25' x 20'
two-car
garage

Features

- Colonnade entry opens to a vaulted foyer with unique dual-access staircase; stairs split at a common landing, one leads to the kitchen, the other curves to the foyer.
- Foyer, with plant ledges above, open to the living and dining rooms; sliding glass doors beyond open to a patio.
- Kitchen with ample counter preparation area

serves the bay windowed breakfast area.
- Half-wall separates the breakfast bay from the vaulted family room.
- Master bedroom boasts a walk-in closet, corner-positioned whirlpool spa and shower.
- Second bedroom resting in a large windowed bay provides a 180-degree view.

Total Living Area: 2,270 sq. ft.

PRICE CODE: C

CUSTOMIZE IT!

ORDER TOLL FREE 1■800■533■4350   **24-HOUR FAX ORDERING** 1■800■344■4293

PLAN FD5275

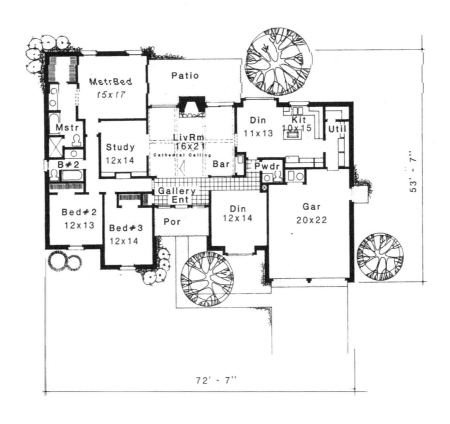

Total Living Area   2,277 sq. ft.

PRICE CODE: C

PLAN DB1771

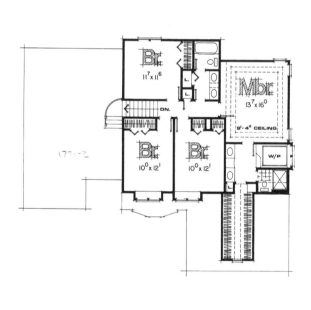

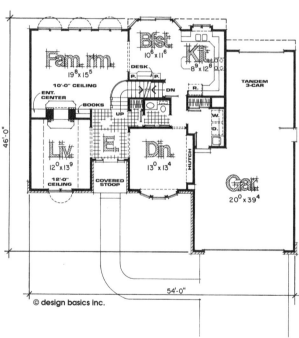

© design basics inc.

Features

- Expansive entry views to arched transom windows in family room.
- Volume ceilings in entry, family room and living room .
- Bayed windows and hutch space in dining room.
- Powder bath located for dual access.
- See-thru fireplace serves both living room and family room.

- Island kitchen adjoins sunny dinette with built-in desk.
- Well-equipped laundry.
- Secondary bedrooms served by compartmented bath with double vanity and large linen closet.
- Tiered ceiling in large master bedroom.
- Master bath with 2-person whirlpool and huge walk-in closet.

First Floor	**1,204 sq. ft.**
Second Floor	**1,075 sq. ft.**
Total Living Area	**2,279 sq. ft.**

PRICE CODE: D

CUSTOMIZE IT!

ORDER TOLL FREE 1■800■533■4350   24-HOUR FAX ORDERING 1■800■344■4293

SECOND FLOOR

- MASTER BEDROOM 16'-6" x 12'-6"
- MASTER BATH
- BEDROOM #3 10'-0" x 10'-9"
- OPEN TO FAMILY ROOM BELOW
- D. W.
- DN.
- BEDROOM #4 10'-0" x 10'-0"
- BATH
- BEDROOM #2 12'-6" x 13'-6"
- OPEN TO ENTRY BELOW

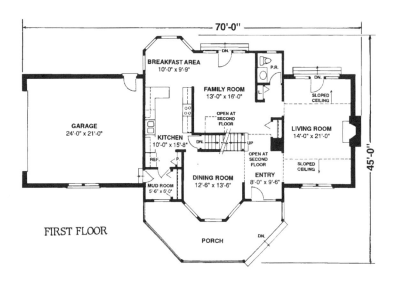

FIRST FLOOR

- 70'-0"
- 45'-0"
- GARAGE 24'-0" x 21'-0"
- BREAKFAST AREA 10'-0" x 9'-9"
- FAMILY ROOM 13'-0" x 16'-0"
- OPEN AT SECOND FLOOR
- P.R.
- SLOPED CEILING
- KITCHEN 10'-0" x 15'-8"
- LIVING ROOM 14'-0" x 21'-0"
- REF.
- UP
- DN.
- OPEN AT SECOND FLOOR
- SLOPED CEILING
- MUD ROOM 5'-6" x 6'-0"
- DINING ROOM 12'-6" x 13'-6"
- ENTRY 8'-0" x 9'-6"
- PORCH
- DN.

Features

- Here's a beautiful Victorian with large living spaces for family activities and entertaining friends.
- Double entry doors lead into an open ceiling foyer with the formal dining room on the left and very spacious sloped ceiling living room with fireplace on the right.
- Upstairs you'll be pleased to find a large master bedroom served by double vanity master bath with linen closet, walk-in closet, and private water closet/shower area.
- Three other upstairs bedrooms share a full bath and laundry room.

First Floor	1,231 sq. ft.
Second Floor	1,049 sq. ft.
Total Living Area	2,280 sq. ft.

PRICE CODE: C

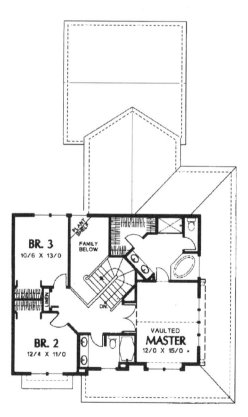

BR. 3
10/6 X 13/0

FAMILY
BELOW

PLANT
SHELF

LINEN

DN

BR. 2
12/4 X 11/0

VAULTED
MASTER
12/0 X 15/0 +

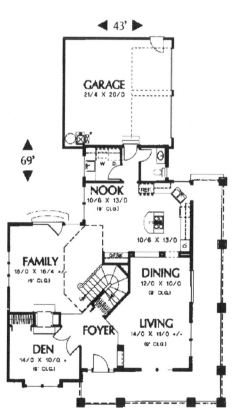

◀ 43' ▶

GARAGE
21/4 X 20/0

W D

69'

NOOK
10/6 X 13/0
(9' CLG.)

REF

10/6 X 13/0

FAMILY
15/0 X 16/4 +/-
(9' CLG.)

DESK

DINING
12/0 X 10/0
(9' CLG.)

FOYER

LIVING
14/0 X 11/0 +/-
(9' CLG.)

DEN
14/0 X 10/0 +
(9' CLG.)

First Floor	1,371 sq. ft.
Second Floor	916 sq. ft.
Total Living Area	2,287 sq. ft.

PRICE CODE: C

CUSTOMIZE IT!

ORDER TOLL FREE 1■800■533■4350   **24-HOUR FAX ORDERING** 1■800■344■4293

PLAN AM2281

◀ 54' ▶

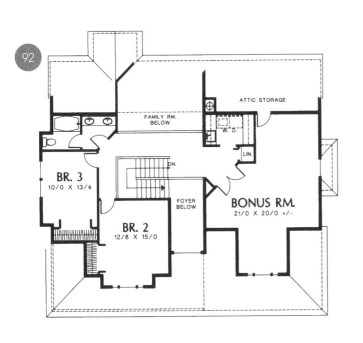

BR. 3
10/0 X 13/4

BR. 2
12/8 X 15/0

FAMILY RM. BELOW

ATTIC STORAGE

W. D.

LIN.

DN.

FOYER BELOW

BONUS RM.
21/0 X 20/0 +/-

▲
49'
▼

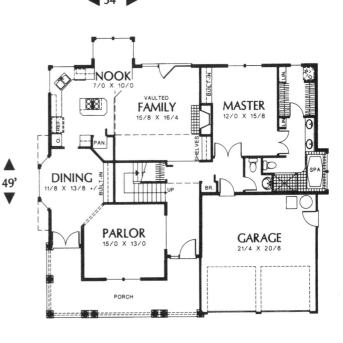

NOOK
7/0 X 10/0

VAULTED
FAMILY
15/8 X 16/4

MASTER
12/0 X 15/8

BUILT-IN

REF.

O.

PAN.

SHELVES

SPA

DINING
11/8 X 13/8

BUILT-IN

UP

BR.

PARLOR
15/0 X 13/0

GARAGE
21/4 X 20/8

PORCH

First Floor	1,587 sq. ft.
Second Floor	716 sq. ft.
Total Living Area	2,303 sq. ft.
Bonus Room	+427 sq. ft.

PRICE CODE: C

92

93

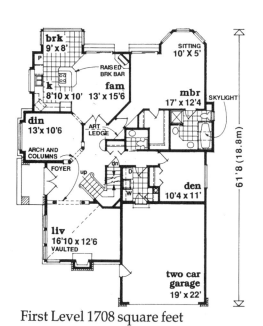

First Level 1708 square feet

Second Level 639 square feet

Features

- Ideal for a corner lot.
- Portico entry opens to a vaulted foyer brightly lit by a multipaned transom window.
- Living room's high vaulted ceiling is accentuated by a series of windows with arched transoms.
- Main floor master bedroom boasts a cozy sitting bay, walk-in closet and ensuite with his and hers vanity, shower and skylit spa.
- Kitchen offers a centre cooking island with raised bar, adjoining breakfast area and spacious family room with sliding glass ,walk-through to the garden patio and corner-positioned fireplace.
- Bonus room provides an additional 330 square feet and may be used as an extra bedroom or games room.

| Total Living Area | 2,347 sq. ft. |

PRICE CODE: C

CUSTOMIZE IT!

ORDER TOLL FREE   1▪800▪533▪4350   24-HOUR FAX ORDERING   1▪800▪344▪4293

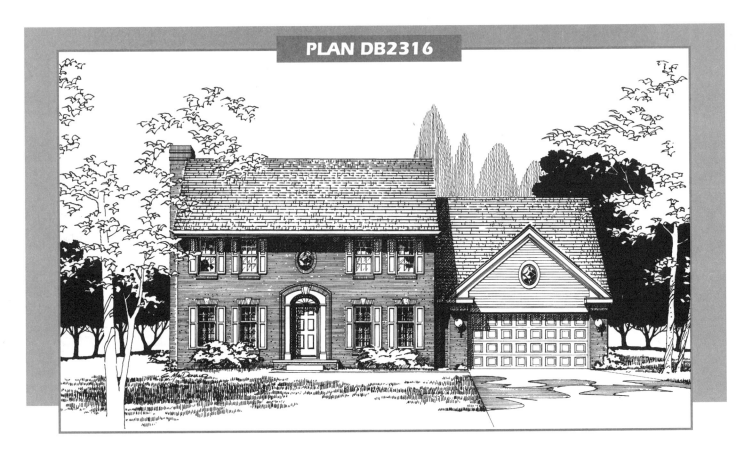

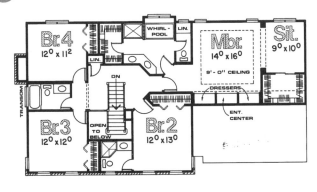

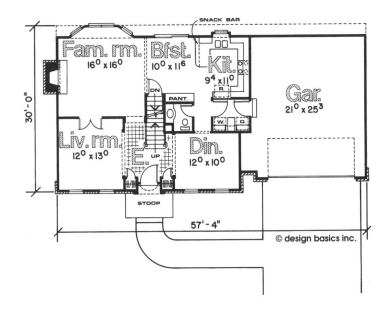

© design basics inc.

Features

- Stately 2-story brick elevation with attractive colonial detailing.
- Formal dining room with convenient passage to kitchen.
- Family room with bayed conversation area includes cozy fireplace.
- Kitchen/dinette area has wrapping counters, snack bar and large pantry.

- Comfortable secondary bedrooms; bedroom #2 enjoys private bath.
- Sumptuous master suite with bookcases, entertainment center, sitting room and large walk-in closet.
- Pampering master bath and dressing area includes angled his and her vanities, whirlpool and second walk-in closet.

First Floor	1,000 sq. f
Second Floor	1,345 sq. f
Total Living Area	2,345 sq. f

PRICE CODE: D

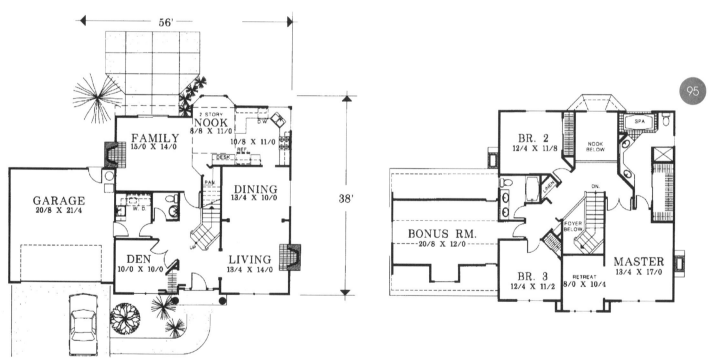

First Floor	1,236 sq. ft.
Second Floor	1,120 sq. ft.
Total Living Area	2,356 sq. ft.
Bonus Room	+270 sq. ft.

PRICE CODE: C

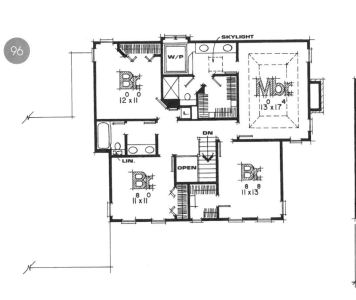

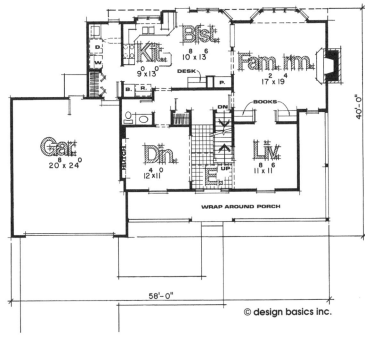

© design basics inc.

Features

- Formal entertaining rooms to the front of the home flanking hard-surfaced entry.
- Family room located for privacy includes bookcases, bayed window and fireplace.
- Main floor powder bath conveniently located, yet discrete.
- Island kitchen is well-planned with wrapping counter, broom closet, pantry and planning desk

plus breakfast area open to family room.
- Huge laundry/mud room has utility sink, coat closet and iron-a-way.
- Island kitchen is well-planned with wrapping counter, broom closet, pantry and planning desk plus breakfast area open to family room.

First Floor	1,188 sq.
Second Floor	1,172 sq.
Total Living Area	2,360 sq.

PRICE CODE: D

SECOND FLOOR

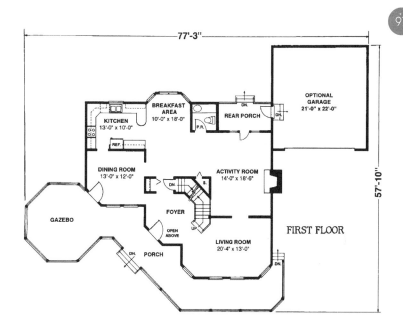

Castlewood

Features

- Country Victorian design with stunning exterior visual appeal.
- Geometric shapes delight the senses, with a spectacular octagonal gazebo.
- Large activity room with fireplace and access to rear covered porch.

- Dining room opens out to gazebo for inside/outside entertaining.
- Upstairs, an enormous master bedroom has a sitting area, his/her walk-through closets, and master bath with private water closet.
- Two additional bedrooms share a full bath.

First Floor	1,281 sq. ft.
Second Floor	1,089 sq. ft.
Total Living Area	2,370 sq. ft.

PRICE CODE: C

CUSTOMIZE IT!

ORDER TOLL FREE 1 ▪ 800 ▪ 533 ▪ 4350   **24-HOUR FAX ORDERING** 1 ▪ 800 ▪ 344 ▪ 4293

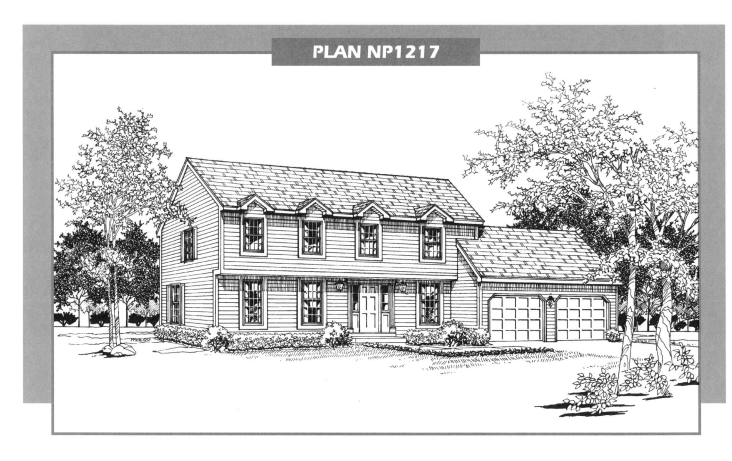

SECOND FLOOR

Second floor rooms:
- BEDROOM 12'x12'-6"
- BEDROOM 12'x15'-6"
- BEDROOM 12'x12'-2"
- MASTER BEDROOM 12'x18'-8"

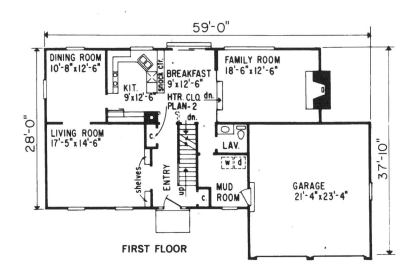

FIRST FLOOR

First floor rooms:
- DINING ROOM 10'-8"x12'-6"
- KIT. 9'x12'-6"
- BREAKFAST 9'x12'-6"
- FAMILY ROOM 18'-6"x12'-6"
- LIVING ROOM 17'-5"x14'-6"
- HTR. CLO. PLAN-2
- LAV.
- MUD ROOM
- GARAGE 21'-4"x23'-4"
- ENTRY
- shelves

Dimensions: 59'-0", 28'-0", 37'-10"

Early American Heritage

Features

- Exterior features of this Early American home showcase its unique design.
- Second-floor overhang and gabled windows add dramatic tension to horizontal siding.
- Formal dining room is located to the left of the kitchen.
- Large sunken family room includes fireplace.
- Second-floor includes master bedroom, deluxe master bath with corner deck tub and double vanity, and large walk-in closet.
- Three additional upstairs bedrooms share a full bath.

First Floor	1,212 sq. ft.
Second Floor	1,160 sq. ft.
Total Living Area	2,372 sq. ft.

PRICE CODE: C

CUSTOMIZE IT!

ORDER TOLL FREE **1■800■533■4350**   24-HOUR FAX ORDERING **1■800■344■4293**

PLAN AM2271

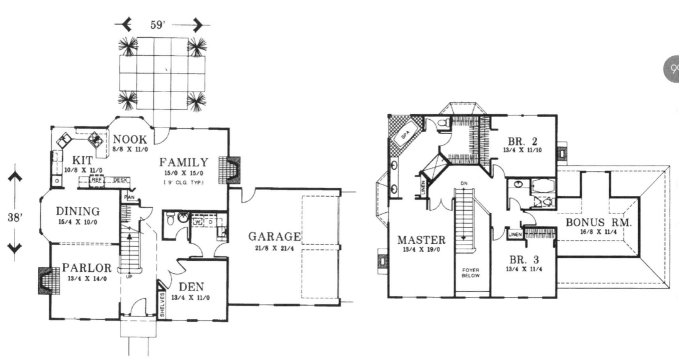

59'

38'

NOOK
8/8 X 11/0

KIT
10/8 X 11/0

FAMILY
15/0 X 15/0
[9' CLG. TYP.]

REF   DESK

PAN

DINING
15/4 X 10/0

GARAGE
21/8 X 21/4

PARLOR
13/4 X 14/0

UP

DEN
13/4 X 11/0

SHELVES

SPA

BR. 2
13/4 X 11/10

LINEN

DN

MASTER
13/4 X 19/0

LINEN

LINEN

BONUS RM.
16/8 X 11/4

BR. 3
13/4 X 11/4

FOYER
BELOW

First Floor	1,285 sq. ft.
Second Floor	1,100 sq. ft.
Total Living Area	2,385 sq. ft.
Bonus Room	+238 sq. ft.

PRICE CODE: C

CUSTOMIZE IT!

ORDER TOLL FREE   1■800■533■4350   24-HOUR FAX ORDERING   1■800■344■4293

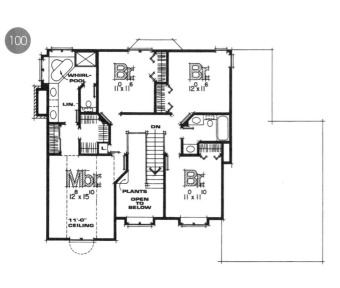

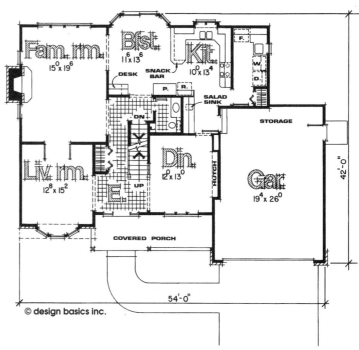

© design basics inc.

Features

- Bright 2-story entry with plant shelf.
- Hard surface trafficways.
- Central hall formalizes front half of the house.
- French doors connect family room and living room with enticing bayed window.
- Efficient kitchen with snack bar and pantry is open to bayed breakfast area with planning desk.
- Salad sink and counter space doubles as servery for formal dining room.
- Master bedroom offers volume ceiling and arched window.
- Master bath features walk-through closet/transition area and corner whirlpool.
- Interesting angles add design character to bedrooms.

First Floor	1,303 sq. f
Second Floor	1,084 sq. f
Total Living Area	2,387 sq. f

PRICE CODE: D

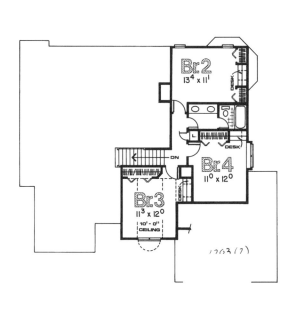

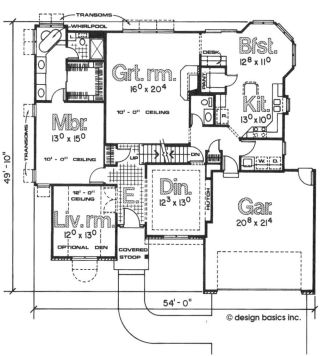

101

Features

- Entry flanked by formal rooms.
- French doors open into volume living room/ optional den with dramatic arched window under volume ceiling.
- 2-sided fireplace for the large great room and windows out the back.
- Formal ceiling and hutch space in dining room.
- Walk-in pantry, desk and island counter in kitchen

open to semi-gazebo dinette.
- Convenient access to laundry room with soaking sink and window.
- Luxurious master dressing/bath area features his and her vanities, walk-in closet and corner whirlpool under windows.
- Built-in desk for each secondary bedroom.
- Compartmented bath for second level.

First Floor	1,697 sq. ft.
Second Floor	694 sq. ft.
Total Living Area	2,391 sq. ft.

PRICE CODE: D

CUSTOMIZE IT!

PLAN FD6922-L

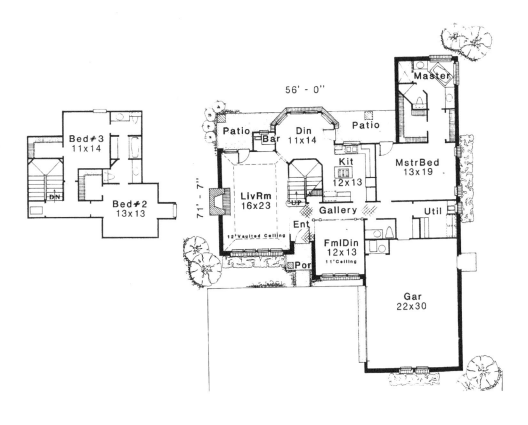

Bed#3
11x14

Bed#2
13x13

DN

56' - 0''

71' - 7''

Patio

Din
11x14

Bar

Patio

Master

Kit
12x13

MstrBed
13x19

LivRm
16x23

UP

Gallery

Util

12'Vaulted Ceiling

Ent

FmlDin
12x13

11'Ceiling

Por

Gar
22x30

First Floor	1,755 sq. ft.
Second Floor	647 sq. ft.
Total Living Area	2,402 sq. ft.

PRICE CODE: C

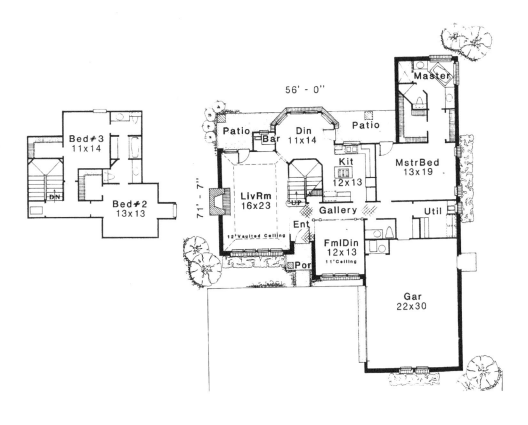

102

103

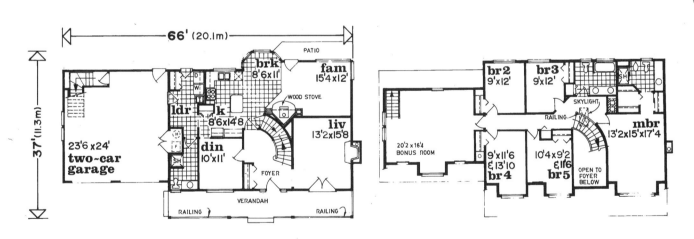

Features

- Five bedrooms and bonus room – ideal for a growing family.
- Vaulted foyer spills to the living room; French doors open to the covered verandah.
- Island kitchen, with pantry and abundant counters, adjoins the breakfast bay.
- Family room is warmed by a cozy wood stove.
- Master bedroom offers a dormer window sitting area, walk-in and wall closets and ensuite with shower.
- Main bath has twin vanity and soaking tub.
- Bonus room, with private stairway access, provides an additional 352 square feet.

Total Living Area   **2,409 sq. ft.**

PRICE CODE: C

CUSTOMIZE IT!

ORDER TOLL FREE   1■800■533■4350   24-HOUR FAX ORDERING   1■800■344■4293

BEDROOM
12' x 13'-6"

BEDROOM
13' x 12'-4"

closet

BEDROOM
12' x 13'-6"

MASTER
BEDROOM
13' x 17'-4"

dn.
open

BATH

roof

38'-0"

33'-0"

SECOND FLOOR

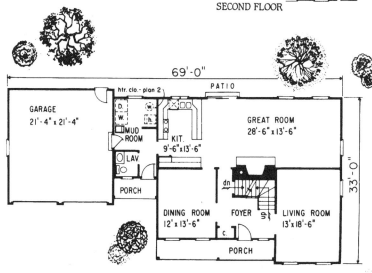

69'-0"

GARAGE
21'-4" x 21'-4"

PATIO

htr. clo.- plan 2

MUD
ROOM

KIT.
9'-6"x13'-6"

GREAT ROOM
28'-6" x 13'-6"

LAV.

PORCH

DINING ROOM
12' x 13'-6"

FOYER

LIVING ROOM
13'x18'-6"

dn

up

PORCH

33'-0"

FIRST FLOOR PLAN 1 WITH BASEMENT
FIRST FLOOR PLAN 2 WITHOUT BASEMENT

Victorian Flair

Features

- Two-story, country Victorian home makes every bit of floor space count.
- Central foyer features an L-shaped staircase, and access to living and dining rooms.
- Huge great room with fireplace at rear of home has sliding glass door access to backyard patio.
- Informal porch entry leads to lavatory/mud room and garage.
- Second-floor master bedroom includes private, full bath.
- Three additional bedrooms share a full bath with double-vanity

First Floor	1,282 sq. ft.
Second Floor	1,132 sq. ft.
Total Living Area	2,414 sq. ft.

PRICE CODE: C

SECOND FLOOR

Second floor rooms:
- BEDROOM 12' x 13'-6"
- BEDROOM 13' x 12'-4"
- BEDROOM 12' x 13'-6"
- MASTER BEDROOM 13' x 17'-4"
- BATH
- closet
- roof

38'-0"

33'-0"

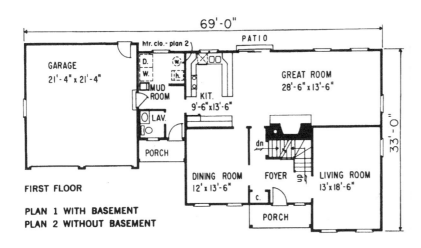

FIRST FLOOR

PLAN 1 WITH BASEMENT
PLAN 2 WITHOUT BASEMENT

First floor rooms:
- GARAGE 21'-4" x 21'-4"
- htr. clo. - plan 2
- PATIO
- GREAT ROOM 28'-6" x 13'-6"
- MUD ROOM
- KIT. 9'-6" x 13'-6"
- LAV.
- PORCH
- DINING ROOM 12' x 13'-6"
- FOYER
- LIVING ROOM 13' x 18'-6"
- PORCH

69'-0"

33'-0"

105

Early American Domain

Features

- Two-story with Early American flair offers no-nonsense layout that makes every bit of floor space count.
- Covered porch entrance into foyer that showcases L-shaped stairs.
- Great room at rear of house features a fireplace and sliding glass door access to patio.
- U-shaped kitchen adjoins formal dining room.
- Informal porch entry leads to lavatory/mud room with access to garage.
- Second-floor master bedroom with private bath.
- Three large bedrooms upstairs share full bath.

First Floor	1,282 sq. ft.
Second Floor	1,132 sq. ft.
Total Living Area	2,414 sq. ft.

PRICE CODE: C

PLAN FD7756A

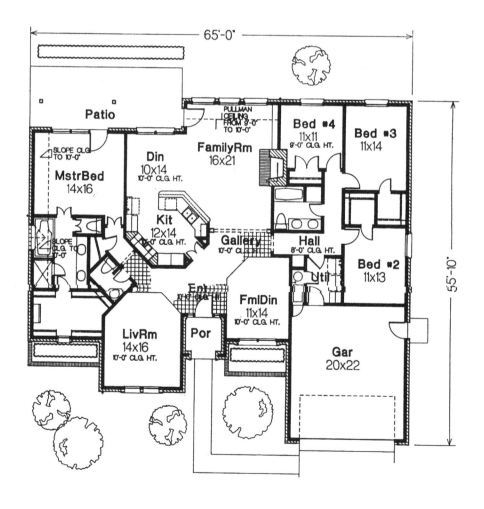

Total Living Area   2,425 sq. ft.

PLAN DB2702

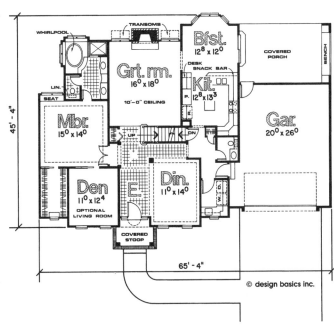

© design basics inc.

Features

- Colonial elevation makes comfortable yet impressive statement.
- Formal dining room defined by ceiling treatment and flooring materials.
- Great room features beautiful windows flanking fireplace.
- Kitchen features wrap-around counter with lazy Susan, large pantry, handy desk and island.

- Double doors open to majestic master bedroom with window seat.
- Pocket door accesses private den from master bedroom.
- Pampering master bath is accentuated by whirlpool, shower and dual lavs.
- Secondary bedrooms share convenient compartmented bath.

First Floor	1,716 sq. ft.
Second Floor	716 sq. ft.
Total Living Area	2,432 sq. ft.

PRICE CODE: D

CUSTOMIZE IT!

ORDER TOLL FREE   1 ■ 800 ■ 533 ■ 4350   24-HOUR FAX ORDERING   1 ■ 800 ■ 344 ■ 4293

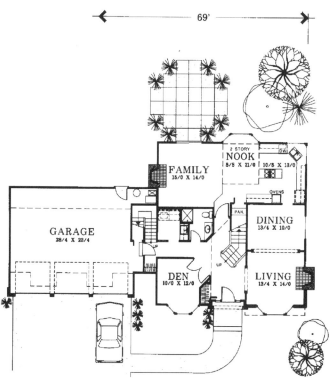

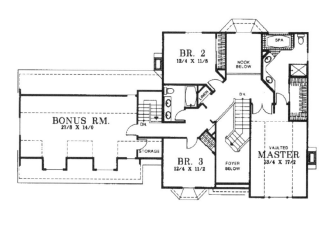

First Floor	1,360 sq. ft.
Second Floor	1,082 sq. ft.
Total Living Area	2,442 sq. ft.
Bonus Room	+482 sq. ft.

PRICE CODE: C

PLAN FD7143-L

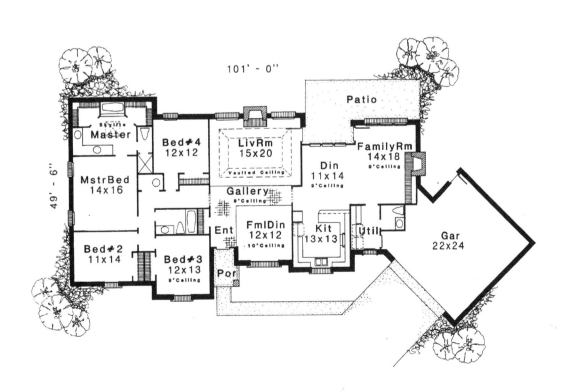

101' - 0''

49' - 6''

Patio

Master

skylite

MstrBed
14x16

Bed#2
11x14

Bed#4
12x12

Bed#3
12x13
9'Ceiling

Ent

Por

LivRm
15x20
Vaulted Ceiling

Gallery
9'Ceiling

FmlDin
12x12
10'Ceiling

Din
11x14
9'Ceiling

Kit
13x13

Util

FamilyRm
14x18
9'Ceiling

Gar
22x24

Total Living Area   2,459 sq. ft.

PRICE CODE: C

CUSTOMIZE IT!

ORDER TOLL FREE   1▪800▪533▪4350   24-HOUR FAX ORDERING   1▪800▪344▪4293

PLAN FD6970

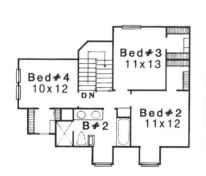

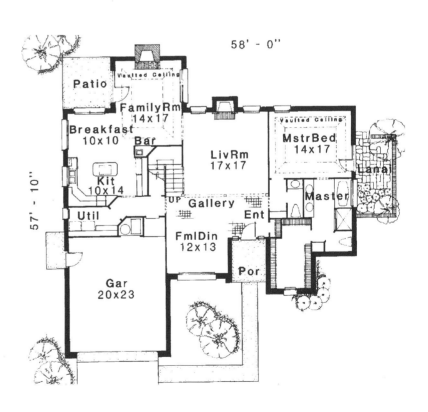

First Floor	1,805 sq. ft.
Second Floor	659 sq. ft.
Total Living Area	2,464 sq. ft.

PRICE CODE: C

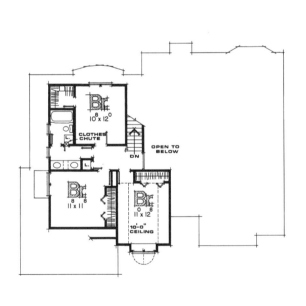

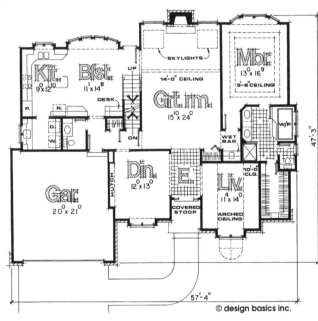

111

Features

- Dining room with hutch space off entry.
- Volume living room has arched ceiling.
- Laundry room near kitchen with clothes chute.
- Convenient powder bath location.
- Island kitchen with pantry.
- Bright bowed breakfast area .
- Large great room with skylights illuminating fireplace.
- Wet bar serves informal living areas.
- Upstairs hall overlooking great room.
- Large master bedroom with sitting bayed window.
- Spacious compartmented bathroom for secondary bedrooms.

First Floor	1,765 sq. ft.
Second Floor	704 sq. ft.
Total Living Area	2,469 sq. ft.

PRICE CODE: D

CUSTOMIZE IT!

ORDER TOLL FREE 1■800■533■4350 24-HOUR FAX ORDERING 1■800■344■4293

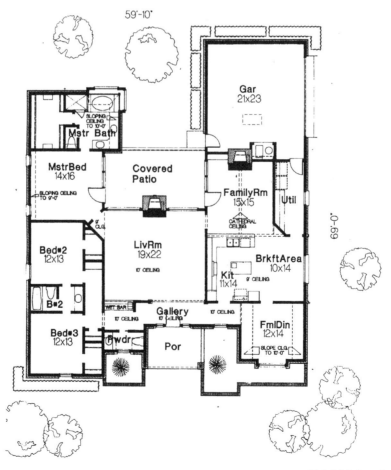

59'-10"

69'-0"

Gar
21x23

Mstr Bath

MstrBed
14x16

**Covered
Patio**

FamilyRm
15x15

Util

Bed#2
12x13

LivRm
19x22

BrkftArea
10x14

Kit
11x14

B#2

WET BAR

Gallery

FmlDin
12x14

Bed#3
12x13

Pwdr

Por

Total Living Area   2,470 sq. ft.

CUSTOMIZE IT!

PLAN FD7904-L

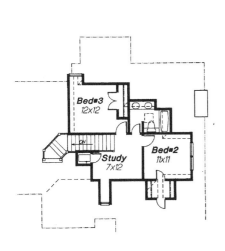

Bed#3
12x12

Study
7x12

Bed#2
11x11

58'-10"

MstrBed
14x17

Patio

Din
10x11

Patio

LivRm
12x15

Kit
11x14

FamilyRm
17x18

Gallery

Stor

Bed#4
/Study
10x10

Ent

Por

FmlDin
11x12

Util

Gar
20x24

60'-9"

© Copyright Fillmore Design Group

First Floor	1,976 sq. ft.
Second Floor	517 sq. ft.
Total Living Area	2,493 sq. ft.

PRICE CODE: C

CUSTOMIZE IT!

ORDER TOLL FREE   1■800■533■4350   24-HOUR FAX ORDERING   1■800■344■4293

PLAN FD7056-LA

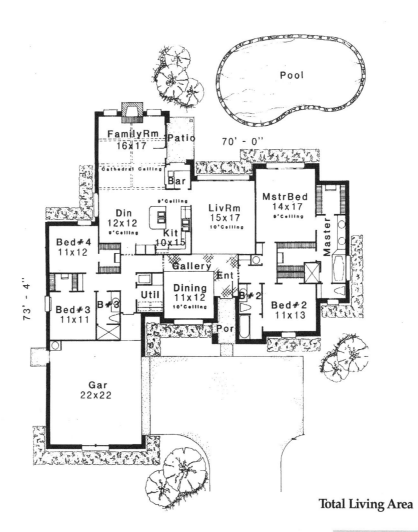

Pool

FamilyRm
16x17

Patio

Cathedral Ceiling

Bar

70' - 0"

MstrBed
14x17
9'Ceiling

Din
12x12
9'Ceiling

LivRm
15x17
10'Ceiling

Master

9'Ceiling

Kit
10x15

Bed #4
11x12

Gallery

Ent

73' - 4"

Util

Dining
11x12
10'Ceiling

B #2

Bed #2
11x13

Bed #3
11x11

B #3

Por

Gar
22x22

Total Living Area   2,495 sq. ft.

PRICE CODE: C

CUSTOMIZE IT!

ORDER TOLL FREE   **1▪800▪533▪4350**   24-HOUR FAX ORDERING   **1▪800▪344▪4293**

PLAN NP1210

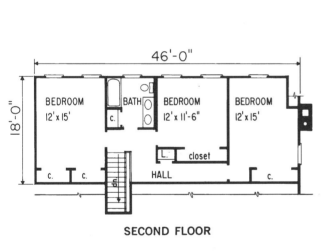

SECOND FLOOR

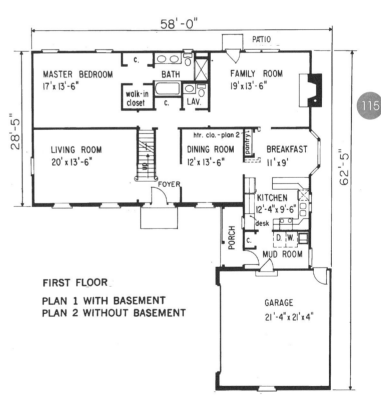

FIRST FLOOR

PLAN 1 WITH BASEMENT
PLAN 2 WITHOUT BASEMENT

115

Elegante

Features

- Colonial design adds a distinctive touch to this two-story.
- Porch opens into mud room and kitchen with adjoining breakfast nook.
- Front door opens into a foyer with adjoining living room and dining room.
- First floor master bedroom with private bathroom.
- Large family room with fireplace and rear patio.
- Second floor features three bedrooms.

First Floor	1,702 sq. ft.
Second Floor	816 sq. ft.
Total Living Area	2,518 sq. ft.

PRICE CODE: C

CUSTOMIZE IT!

ORDER TOLL FREE 1■800■533■4350   24-HOUR FAX ORDERING 1■800■344■4293

PLAN MN2537

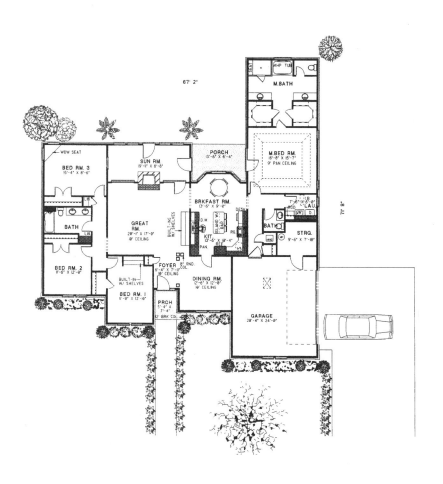

Total Living Area   **2,537 sq. ft.**

PRICE CODE: C

CUSTOMIZE IT!

ORDER TOLL FREE   1■800■533■4350   24-HOUR FAX ORDERING   1■800■344■4293

PLAN FD7969-L

Attic Storage

Loft
17x10
7'-0" clg.

Bonus Room
30x17
9'-0" clg.

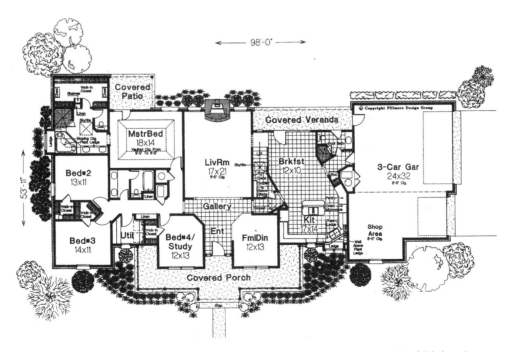

← 98'-0" →

53'-11"

Covered Patio

MstrBed
18x14

Bed#2
13x11

Bed#3
14x11

Bed#4/
Study
12x13

Utility

Ent

Gallery

LivRm
17x21

FmlDin
12x13

Brkfst
12x10

Covered Veranda

Kit
17x14

3-Car Gar
24x32

Shop Area

© Copyright Fillmore Design Group

Covered Porch

Total Living Area   2,539 sq. ft.

PRICE CODE: C

SECOND FLOOR

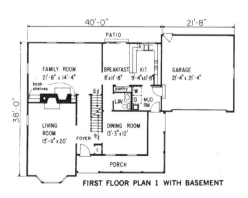

FIRST FLOOR PLAN 1 WITH BASEMENT

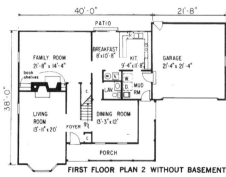

FIRST FLOOR PLAN 2 WITHOUT BASEMENT

Scarborough

Features

- Victorian charm inside and out.
- Elegant covered front porch provides entry to either the main foyer or the mud room.
- One chimney serves cozy back-to-back fireplaces in the living room and family room.
- Sliding door in breakfast area opens to patio.
- Large master bedroom with private bath and three bedrooms with full bath upstairs.

First Floor	1,333 sq. ft.
Second Floor	1,221 sq. ft.
Total Living Area	2,554 sq. ft.

PRICE CODE: C

CUSTOMIZE IT!

ORDER TOLL FREE   1▪800▪533▪4350   24-HOUR FAX ORDERING   1▪800▪344▪4293

PLAN AM2267G

119

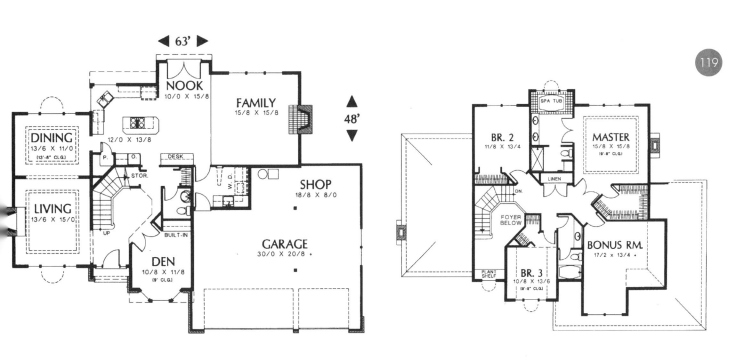

◄ 63' ►

NOOK
10/0 X 15/8

FAMILY
15/8 X 15/8

▲ 48' ▼

DINING
13/6 X 11/0
(13'-8" CLG.)

12/0 X 13/8

P.   O.
STOR.
DESK

SHOP
18/8 X 8/0

LIVING
13/6 X 15/0

W. D.

BUILT-IN

UP

GARAGE
30/0 X 20/8 +

DEN
10/8 X 11/8
(9' CLG.)

SPA TUB

BR. 2
11/8 X 13/4

MASTER
15/8 X 15/8
(9'-9" CLG.)

LINEN

DN.

FOYER
BELOW

PLANT
SHELF

BR. 3
10/8 X 13/6
(9'-9" CLG.)

BONUS RM.
17/2 X 13/4

JOHNSTON PUBLIC LIBRARY
JOHNSTON, IOWA 50131

First Floor	1,465 sq. ft.
Second Floor	1,103 sq. ft.
Total Living Area	2,568 sq. ft.
Bonus Room	+303 sq. ft.

PRICE CODE: C

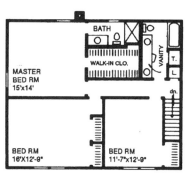

SECOND FLOOR THREE BEDROOMS

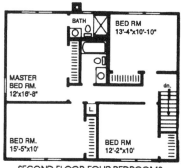

SECOND FLOOR FOUR BEDROOMS

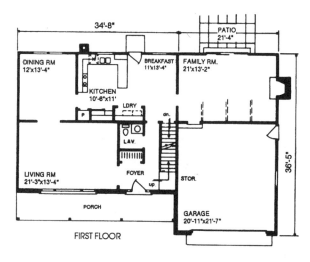

FIRST FLOOR

Homewood

Features

- A covered porch spans the front of this two-story colonial.
- Entry foyer opens to hallway leading to breakfast area served by U-shaped kitchen.
- Large family room with fireplace and beamed ceilings.
- Generously sized living room with mullioned picture window adjoins formal dining room.
- Second-floor option allows either three or four bedrooms with two full baths.

First Floor	**1,288 sq. ft.**
Second Floor	**970 sq. ft.**
Total Living Area	**2,258 sq. ft.**

PRICE CODE: C

CUSTOMIZE IT!

ORDER TOLL FREE   1■800■533■4350   24-HOUR FAX ORDERING   1■800■344■4293

PLAN DB829

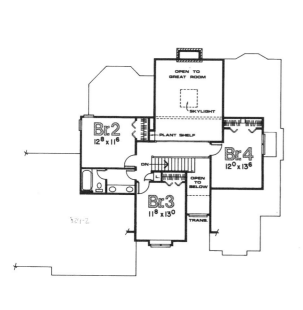

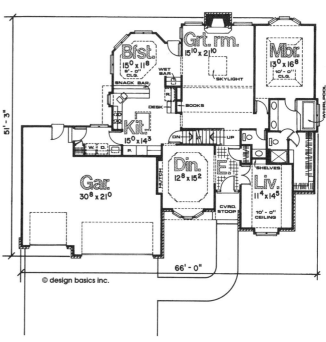

© design basics inc.

121

Features

- Entry open to formal dining room graced with hutch space, special ceiling detail and beautiful bayed window.
- French doors open into formal living room with volume ceiling, glass shelves and bright boxed window.
- Great room features volume sloped ceiling with skylight, built-in bookcase and fireplace framed by windows.

- Island kitchen includes corner sink, pantry, desk and snack bar serving sunny breakfast area with wet bar.
- Master bedroom adorned with vaulted ceiling and bayed window to the back.
- Master dressing/bath area features vanity with lavs, walk-in closet and whirlpool tub hall bath with double vanity.

First Floor	1,748 sq. ft.
Second Floor	834 sq. ft.
Total Living Area	2,582 sq. ft.

PRICE CODE: D

CUSTOMIZE IT!

ORDER TOLL FREE **1 ▪ 800 ▪ 533 ▪ 4350**   24-HOUR FAX ORDERING **1 ▪ 800 ▪ 344 ▪ 4293**

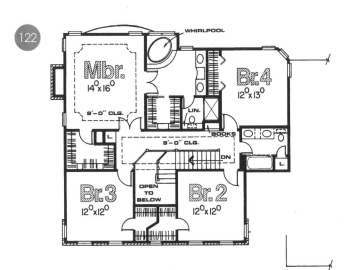

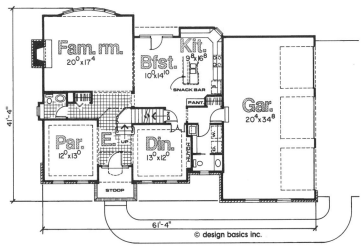

© design basics inc.

61'-4"

Features

- Gracing the elevation of this captivating colonial are decorative windows and brick detailing.
- 9-foot-high main level walls.
- Half bath off laundry area.
- Formal dining room is complemented by French doors, distinctive ceiling treatment and space to accommodate your buffet or hutch.
- Family room brightened by airy bowed window .

- Spacious kitchen provides large pantry, snack bar and abundant food preparation surface area.
- A resplendent master suite presents all of the most desirable amenities.

First Floor	1,362 sq.
Second Floor	1,223 sq.
Total Living Area	2,585 sq.

PRICE CODE: D

CUSTOMIZE IT!

ORDER TOLL FREE 1▪800▪533▪4350   24-HOUR FAX ORDERING   1▪800▪344▪4293

123

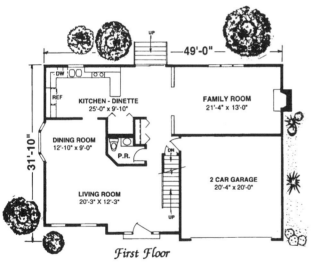

First Floor

Second Floor

First Floor	1,168 sq. ft.
Second Floor	1,418 sq. ft.
Total Living Area	2,586 sq. ft.

PRICE CODE: C

124

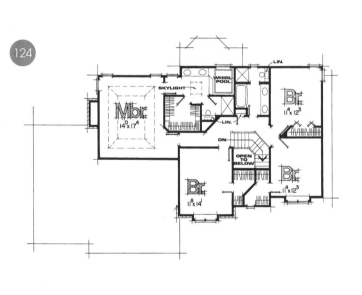

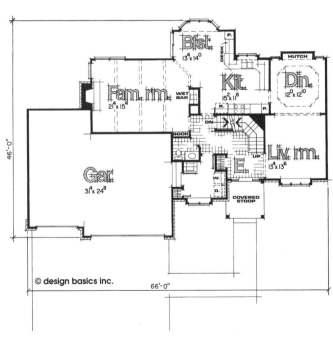

© design basics inc.

Features

- Entry highlighted by angling staircase
- Formal dining room with special ceiling detail and hutch space open to living room for entertaining options.
- Extra storage space in garage.
- Expansive family room with beamed ceiling, bookcase and wet bar highlighted by handsome fireplace.

- Kitchen with wrapping counter, 2 pantries and desk adjoins bayed breakfast area with access to outside.
- Master suite features vaulted ceiling and skylit dressing/bath area with walk-in closet, double vanity and 2-person whirlpool tub.
- Second and third bedrooms include boxed windows and walk-in closets.

First Floor	1,320 sq. ft.
Second Floor	1,270 sq. ft.
Total Living Area	2,590 sq. ft.

PRICE CODE: D

PLAN FD8063-L

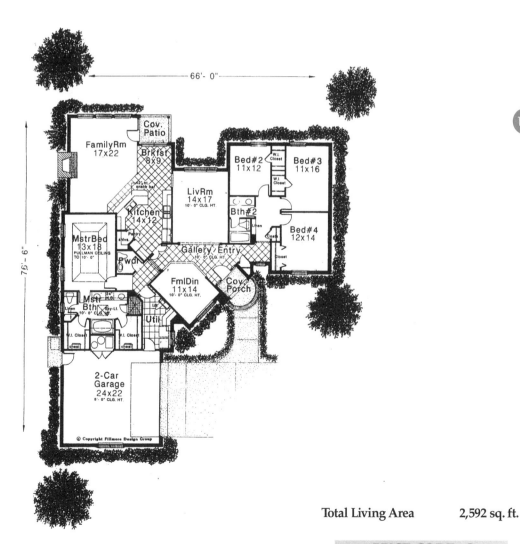

66'- 0"

76'- 6"

Cov. Patio

FamilyRm
17x22

Brkfst
8x9

LivRm
14x17
10'- 0" CLG. HT.

Bed#2
11x12

W.I. Closet

Bed#3
11x16

W.I. Closet

Bth#2

Kitchen
14x12

MstrBed
13x18
PULLMAN CEILING
TO 10'- 0"

Pwdr

Gallery Entry
10'- 0" CLG. HT.

Bed#4
12x14

Mstr Bth
10'- 0" CLG. HT.

FmlDin
11x14
10'- 0" CLG. HT.

Cov. Porch

W.I. Closet

Util

2-Car Garage
24x22
8'- 0" CLG. HT.

© Copyright Fillmore Design Group

125

Total Living Area   2,592 sq. ft.

PRICE CODE: C

126

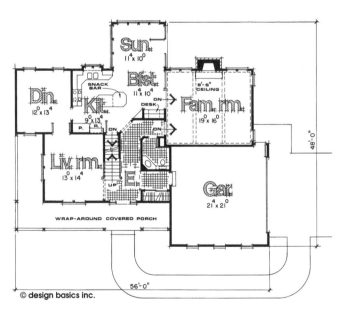

© design basics inc.

Features

- Dreamy wrap-around porch.
- French doors between living room and dining room.
- Island kitchen with snack bar, pantry and lazy Susan.
- Planning desk in dinette adjoining sunroom .
- Sunken family room with beamed ceiling and fireplace located in back for multiple furniture arrangements.
- Vaulted ceiling in master bedroom.
- Extra wide hallway with linen closet.
- French doors into spacious master bath with dramatic bayed window at corner whirlpool tub.
- Secondary bedrooms share compartmented hall bath with 2 vanities.
- Optional play area in third bedroom.

First Floor	1,322 sq. f
Second Floor	1,272 sq. f
Total Living Area	2,594 sq. f

PRICE CODE: D

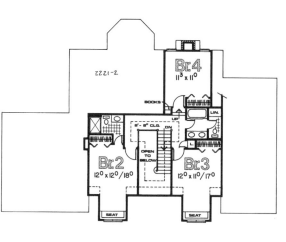

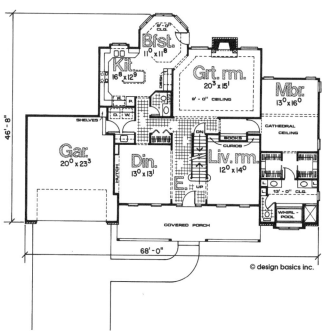

© design basics inc.

127

Features

Large covered front porch.
- Built-in curio cabinets for living room.
- Formal dining room open to a handsome fireplace.
- Kitchen with island counter, pantry, dual lazy Susan and desk.
- Bright gazebo dinette.
- Private hall into master suite features built-in

bookcase.
- Cathedral ceiling in master bedroom.
- Master dressing/bath area with two walk-in closets, his and her vanities and whirlpool under window.
- 2 bath locations for second level.

First Floor	1,780 sq. ft.
Second Floor	815 sq. ft.
Total Living Area	2,595 sq. ft.

PRICE CODE: D

128

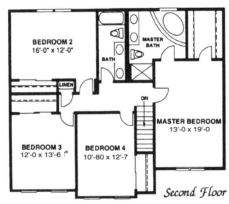

BEDROOM 2
16'-0" x 12'-0"

MASTER BATH

BATH

LINEN

DN

MASTER BEDROOM
13'-0 x 19'-0

BEDROOM 3
12'-0 x 13'-6 !"

BEDROOM 4
10'-80 x 12'-7

Second Floor

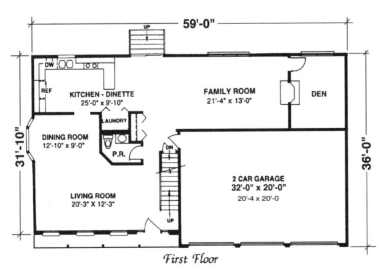

UP

59'-0"

DW

REF

KITCHEN - DINETTE
25'-0" x 9'-10"

FAMILY ROOM
21'-4" x 13'-0"

DEN

LAUNDRY

31'-10"

DINING ROOM
12'-10" x 9'-0"

P.R.

DN

36'-0"

LIVING ROOM
20'-3" X 12'-3"

2 CAR GARAGE
32'-0" x 20'-0"
20'-4 x 20'-0

UP

First Floor

First Floor	1,192 sq. ft.
Second Floor	1,410 sq. ft.
Total Living Area	2,602 sq. ft.

PRICE CODE: C

PLAN FD8037-LB

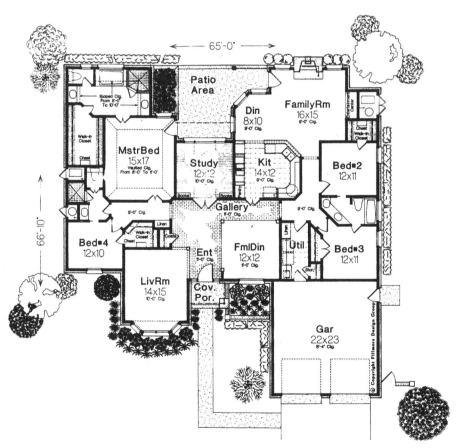

65'-0"

66'-10"

Patio Area

Din 8x10 8'-0" Clg.

FamilyRm 16x15 9'-0" Clg.

MstrBed 15x17 Vaulted Clg. From 8'-0" To 11'-0"

Study 12x12 10'-0" Clg.

Kit 14x12 9'-0" Clg.

Bed #2 12x11 9'-0" Clg.

Walk-in Closet

Bed #4 12x10

Gallery 9'-0" Clg.

FmlDin 12x12 9'-0" Clg.

Util

Bed #3 12x11

Ent

LivRm 14x15 10'-0" Clg.

Cov. Por.

Gar 22x23 8'-4" Clg.

© Copyright Fillmore Design Group

Total Living Area   2,626 sq. ft.

CUSTOMIZE IT!

ORDER TOLL FREE   1■800■533■4350   24-HOUR FAX ORDERING   1■800■344■4293

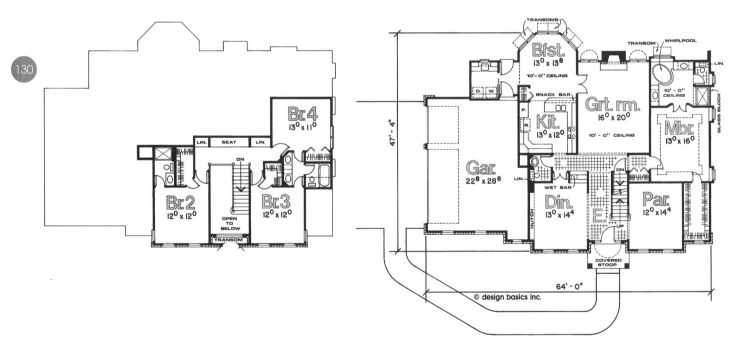

© design basics inc.

Features

- Magnificent brick facade with 3-car side-load garage.
- Kitchen with peninsula adjoins bayed dinette.
- Spacious great room with arched windows gracing fireplace.
- Double-sided wet bar serves formal dining room

and great room.
- French doors lead from master bedroom into bath with angled whirlpool and glass block over shower.
- Reading seat, flanked by 2 cabinets, overlooks staircase and volume entry.

First Floor	1,865 sq. f
Second Floor	774 sq. f
Total Living Area	2,639 sq. f

PRICE CODE: D

CUSTOMIZE IT!

ORDER TOLL FREE 1■800■533■4350 **24-HOUR FAX ORDERING** 1■800■344■4293

PLAN DB2074

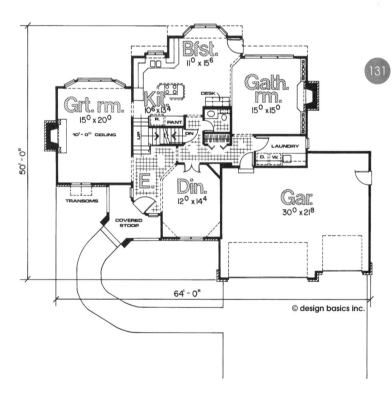

131

© design basics inc.

Features

Many windows brighten 2-story-high wrapping entry.

Fireplace and expansive bayed windows in volume great room visible from entry.

Kitchen features cook top in island, pantry, planning desk and cabinets which wrap into bayed breakfast area.

- Gathering room offers built-in bookcases and second fireplace.
- Master bedroom has formal ceiling and fancy bayed windows.
- Master bath features compartmented shower and stool, bayed windows above corner whirlpool and large skylit walk-in closet.

First Floor	1,407 sq. ft.
Second Floor	1,248 sq. ft.
Total Living Area	2,655 sq. ft.

PRICE CODE: D

CUSTOMIZE IT!

ORDER TOLL FREE 1▪800▪533▪4350   24-HOUR FAX ORDERING 1▪800▪344▪4293

PLAN SH1487-2559

132

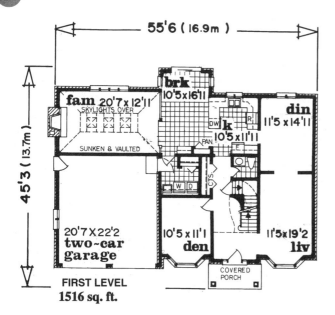

55'6 (16.9m)

45'3 (13.7m)

fam 20'7 x 12'11
SKYLIGHTS OVER

SUNKEN & VAULTED

brk
10'5 x 16'11

k
10'5 x 11'11
DW PAN

din
11'5 x 14'11

W D

20'7 X 22'2
two~car garage

den
10'5 x 11'1

liv
11'5 x 19'2

COVERED
PORCH

**FIRST LEVEL
1516 sq. ft.**

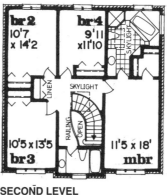

br 2
10'7
x 14'2

br 4
9'11
x 11'10

LINEN

SKYLIGHT

RAILING OPEN

br 3
10'5 x 13'5

mbr
11'5 x 18'

**SECOND LEVEL
1145 sq. ft.**

Features

- Bay windows adorn the living room and den.
- Large breakfast room overlooks the sunken family room.
- Vaulted family room hosts a trio of skylights.
- Curved staircase is brightened by a skylight.
- Railed gallery views the foyer below.
- Skylit ensuite features a raised whirlpool spa.

Total Living Area **2,661 sq. ft.**

PRICE CODE: C

CUSTOMIZE IT!

ORDER TOLL FREE **1 ▪ 800 ▪ 533 ▪ 4350** 24-HOUR FAX ORDERING **1 ▪ 800 ▪ 344 ▪ 4293**

SECOND FLOOR
FOUR BEDROOM PLAN

- Bedroom 13'-7" x 10'
- Bedroom 11'-9" x 16'-6"
- walk in clo.
- DRESS.
- MASTER BEDROOM 14' x 17'-6"
- BATH-2
- Bedroom 15'-4" x 12'-9"

SECOND FLOOR
FIVE BEDROOM PLAN

- BED RM. 11'-11" x 13'-3"
- BED RM. 13'-3" x 9'-11"
- BED RM. 11'-9" x 14'-4"
- BED RM. 11'-11" x 10'-11"
- BATH
- MASTER BED RM. 15'-4" x 16'-3"

133

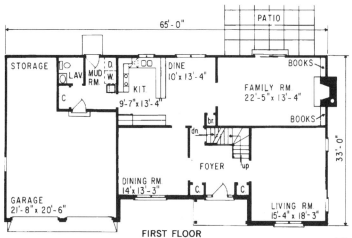

FIRST FLOOR

- 65'-0"
- 33'-0"
- PATIO
- STORAGE
- LAV.
- MUD RM.
- KIT. 9'-7" x 13'-4"
- DINE 10' x 13'-4"
- BOOKS
- FAMILY RM. 22'-5" x 13'-4"
- BOOKS
- FOYER
- DINING RM. 14' x 13'-3"
- LIVING RM. 15'-4" x 18'-3"
- GARAGE 21'-8" x 20'-6"

First Floor	1,398 sq. ft.
Second Floor	1,266 sq. ft.
Total Living Area	2,664 sq. ft.

PRICE CODE: C

CUSTOMIZE IT!

ORDER TOLL FREE 1■800■533■4350   24-HOUR FAX ORDERING 1■800■344■4293

134

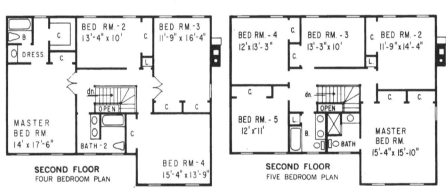

SECOND FLOOR
FOUR BEDROOM PLAN

BED RM.-2
13'-4" x 10'

BED RM.-3
11'-9" x 16'-4"

MASTER BED RM
14' x 17'-6"

BATH-2

BED RM-4
15'-4" x 13'-9"

SECOND FLOOR
FIVE BEDROOM PLAN

BED RM.-4
12' x 13'-3"

BED RM.-3
13'-3" x 10'

BED RM.-2
11'-9" x 14'-4"

BED RM.-5
12' x 11'

BATH

MASTER BED RM.
15'-4" x 15'-10"

Modern Colonial

Features

- This modified colonial design features an 'L' shape that, with the garage on the opposite side, encloses the front porch.
- Main entry into foyer opens to a living room on the right and a formal dining room on the left.
- An informal dining area is adjacent to the kitchen.
- Large family room opens to patio with sliding glass doors and includes a fireplace.
- Second floor includes an option for four or five bedrooms and two full baths.

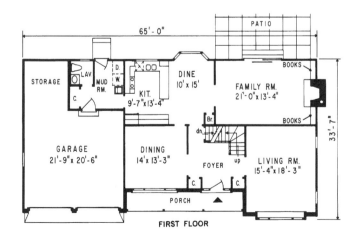

65'-0"

PATIO

STORAGE

LAV

MUD RM.

KIT.
9'-7" x 13'-4"

DINE
10' x 15'

FAMILY RM.
21'-0" x 13'-4"

BOOKS

BOOKS

GARAGE
21'-9" x 20'-6"

DINING
14' x 13'-3"

FOYER

LIVING RM.
15'-4" x 18'-3"

33'-7"

PORCH

FIRST FLOOR

First Floor	1,392 sq. ft.
Second Floor	1,282 sq. ft.
Total Living Area	2,674 sq. ft.

PRICE CODE: C

CUSTOMIZE IT!

ORDER TOLL FREE 1■800■533■4350   24-HOUR FAX ORDERING 1■800■344■4293

PLAN SH1188-2453

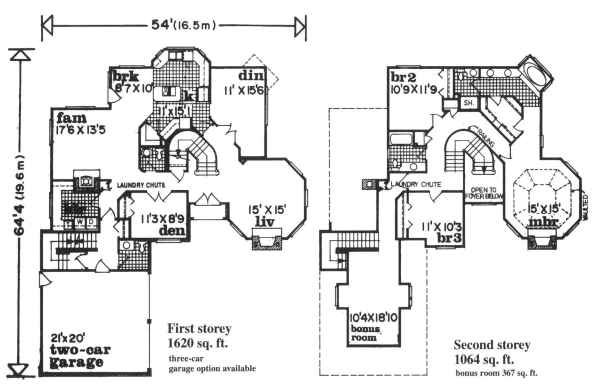

First storey
1620 sq. ft.

three-car
garage option available

Second storey
1064 sq. ft.

bonus room 367 sq. ft.

135

Features

- Sweeping, horseshoe-shaped staircase dominates the two-storey foyer.
- Octagonal living room has a masonry fireplace.
- Kitchen tucked in a bay window is equipped with a walk-in pantry and cooking island.

- Laundry room has a chute from upstairs and sewing counter.
- Coffered ceiling master bedroom features a fireplace and walk-through wardrobe.
- Bonus room, with private staircase, provides an additional 367 square feet of living space.

Total Living Area   2,684 sq. ft.

PRICE CODE: C

CUSTOMIZE IT!

ORDER TOLL FREE   1■800■533■4350   24-HOUR FAX ORDERING   1■800■344■4293

136

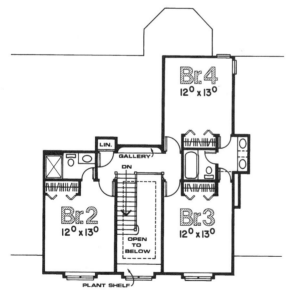

Br.4
12⁰ x 13⁰

LIN.

GALLERY

DN

OPEN TO BELOW

Br.2
12⁰ x 13⁰

Br.3
12⁰ x 13⁰

PLANT SHELF

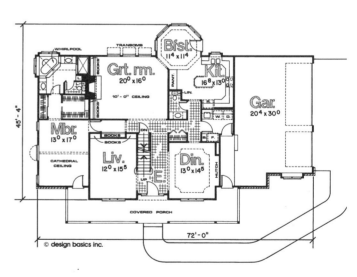

WHIRLPOOL

TRANSOMS

Bfst.
11⁴ x 11⁴

Grt. rm.
20⁰ x 16⁰

10'-0" CEILING

Kit.
16⁸ x 13⁰

Gar.
20⁴ x 30⁰

45'-4"

Mbr.
13⁰ x 17⁰

CATHEDRAL CEILING

BOOKS

Liv.
12⁰ x 15⁵

Din.
13⁰ x 14⁵

COVERED PORCH

72'-0"

© design basics inc.

Features

- Magnificent porch adds appeal to elevation.
- Volume entry surveys formal living and dining rooms.
- Formal living room features two bookcases.
- Impressive great room with three large windows and raised hearth fireplace flanked by bookcases.
- Captivating gazebo dinette and island kitchen with huge pantry and two lazy Susan.
- Upstairs, three secondary bedrooms enjoy ample bathroom accommodations and a gallery in the corridor.
- Main level master suite with porch retreat access, roomy dressing area, his and her vanities and sunlit whirlpool.

First Floor	1,881 sq. ft.
Second Floor	814 sq. ft.
Total Living Area	2,695 sq. ft.

PRICE CODE: D

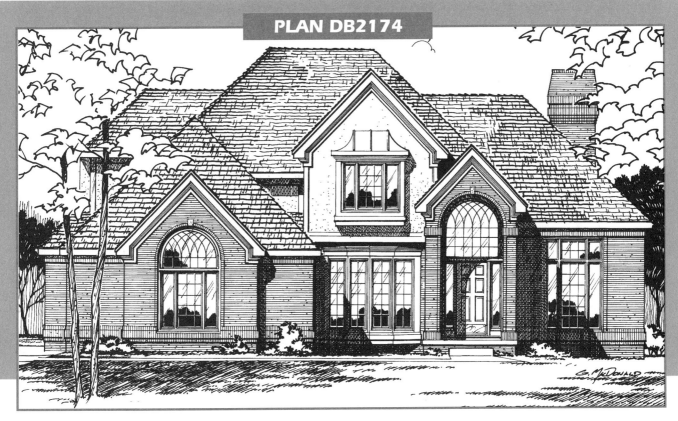

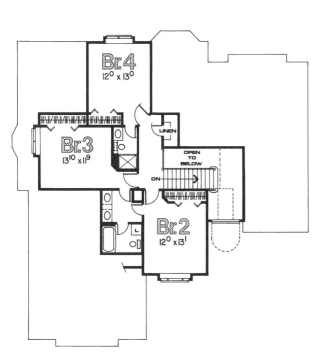

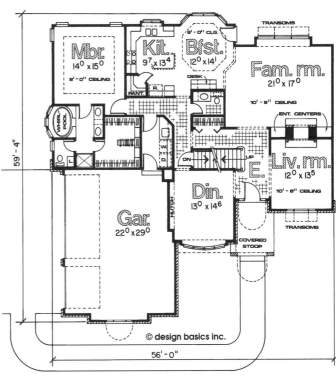

137

Features

- Well proportioned elevation highlighted with repeating gables, elegant crown mould and brick accents.
- 2-story entry boasts large arched transom window.
- Formal dining room offers hutch space and bowed window.

- Living room off entry features volume ceiling and see-thru fireplace.
- Spacious family room has 10'-8" ceiling and dual entertainment centers.
- Octagon, bayed breakfast area compliments island kitchen with walk-in pantry and planning desk.

First Floor	1,860 sq. ft.
Second Floor	848 sq. ft.
Total Living Area	2,708 sq. ft.

PRICE CODE: D

CUSTOMIZE IT!

ORDER TOLL FREE 1 ▪ 800 ▪ 533 ▪ 4350   24-HOUR FAX ORDERING   1 ▪ 800 ▪ 344 ▪ 4293

138

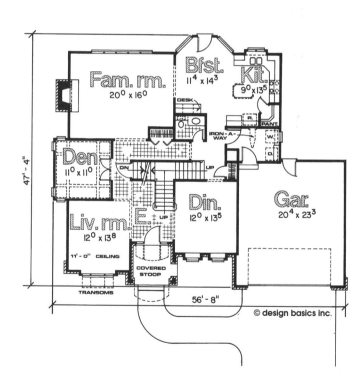

© design basics inc.

Features

- Volume entry views formal dining room and living room.
- T-shaped staircase for efficient traffic flow.
- Double doors into den with spider-beamed ceiling.
- Walk-in corner pantry in island kitchen, family room with raised hearth fireplace and plenty of windows out back.

- Centrally located powder bath to serve main level.
- Formal master suite includes luxurious dressing/bath area with oval whirlpool and plant ledge above.
- Fourth bedroom can become sitting room for master suite.
- Unfinished storage area upstairs.

First Floor	1,521 sq. ft.
Second Floor	1,190 sq. ft.
Total Living Area	2,711 sq. ft.

PRICE CODE: D

CUSTOMIZE IT!

ORDER TOLL FREE   1■800■533■4350   24-HOUR FAX ORDERING   1■800■344■4293

PLAN FD7372

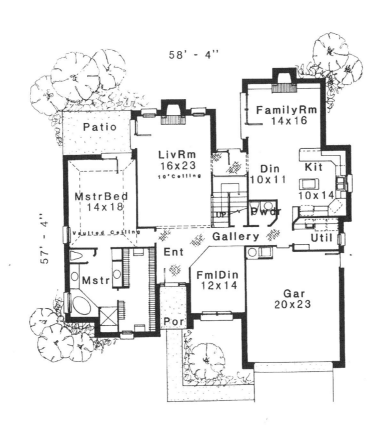

58' - 4''

57' - 4''

Patio

LivRm
16x23
10'Ceiling

FamilyRm
14x16

MstrBed
14x18
Vaulted Ceiling

Din
10x11

Kit
10x14

Mstr

Ent

Gallery

Up

Pwdr

Util

FmlDin
12x14

Gar
20x23

Por

Total Living Area   2,721 sq. ft.

PRICE CODE: C

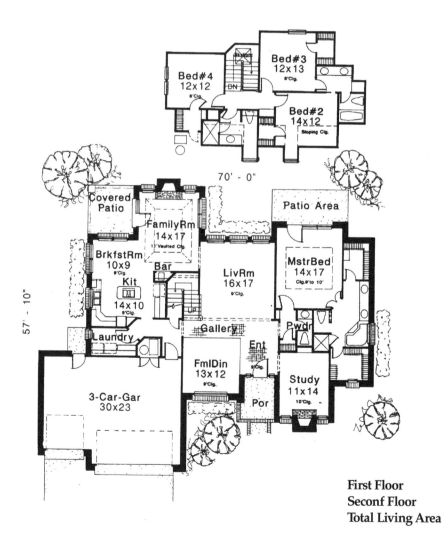

Bed#4
12x12
8'Clg.

Bed#3
12x13
8'Clg.

Bed#2
14x12
Sloping Clg.

DN

70' - 0"

57' - 10"

Covered
Patio

FamilyRm
14x17
11'Vaulted Clg.

Patio Area

BrkfstRm
10x9
9'Clg.

Bar

Kit
14x10
9'Clg.

LivRm
16x17
9'Clg.

MstrBed
14x17
Clg.9'to 10'

UP

Laundry

Gallery

Pwdr

Ent
8'Clg.

3-Car-Gar
30x23

FmlDin
13x12
9'Clg.

Por

Study
11x14
10'Clg.

First Floor	1,960 sq. ft.
Seconf Floor	768 sq. ft.
Total Living Area	2,728 sq. ft.

PRICE CODE: C

140

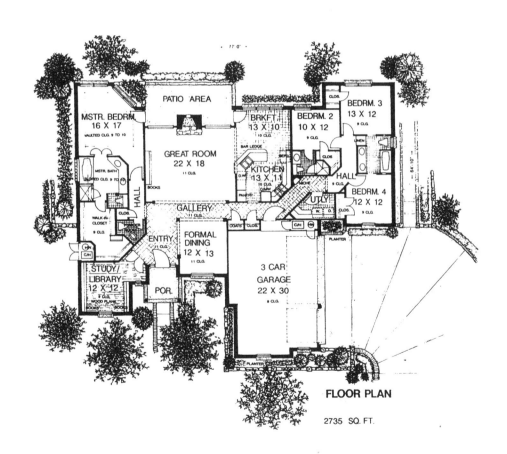

PATIO AREA

MSTR. BEDRM
16 X 17
VAULTED CLG. 9 TO 10

BRKFT.
13 X 10

BEDRM. 2
10 X 12

BEDRM. 3
13 X 12

MSTR. BATH
SLOPED CLG. 9 TO 10

BAR LEDGE

GREAT ROOM
22 X 18
11 CLG.

KITCHEN
13 X 11

HALL

HALL

WALK-IN CLOSET
9 CLG.

GALLERY
11 CLG.

BEDRM. 4
12 X 12

UTLY.

ENTRY
11 CLG.

FORMAL DINING
12 X 13
11 CLG.

3 CAR GARAGE
22 X 30
9 CLG.

STUDY/ LIBRARY
12 X 12
9 CLG.
WOOD PLANK

POR.

PLANTER

FLOOR PLAN

2735 SQ. FT.

Total Living Area	2,735 sq. ft.

PRICE CODE: C

CUSTOMIZE IT!

ORDER TOLL FREE 1■800■533■4350   24-HOUR FAX ORDERING 1■800■344■4293

◄ 70' ►

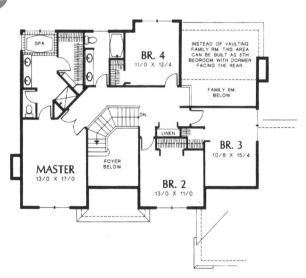

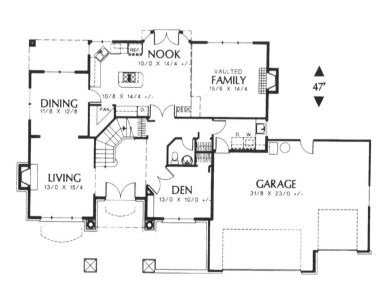

47'

First Floor	1,470 sq. ft.
Second Floor	1,269 sq. ft.
Total Living Area	2,739 sq. ft.

PRICE CODE: C

CUSTOMIZE IT!

ORDER TOLL FREE   **1 ▪ 800 ▪ 533 ▪ 4350**

24-HOUR FAX ORDERING   **1 ▪ 800 ▪ 344 ▪ 4293**

PLAN NPP124

143

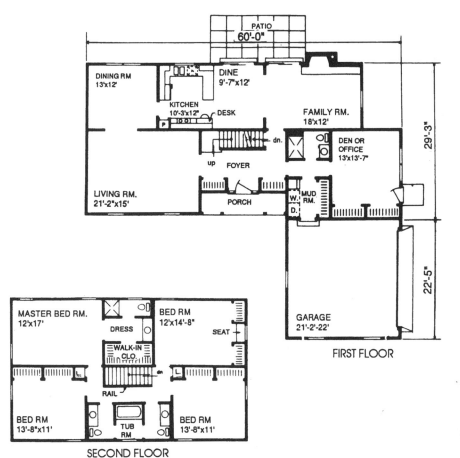

PATIO
60'-0"

DINING RM
13'x12'

DINE
9'-7"x12'

KITCHEN
10'-3"x12'

DESK

FAMILY RM.
18'x12'

DEN OR
OFFICE
13'x13'-7"

up   FOYER

dn.

LIVING RM.
21'-2"x15'

PORCH

W.
D.

MUD
RM.

29'-3"

GARAGE
21'-2'-22'

22'-5"

FIRST FLOOR

MASTER BED RM.
12'x17'

DRESS

BED RM
12'x14'-8"

SEAT

WALK-IN
CLO.

RAIL

BED RM
13'-8"x11'

TUB
RM

BED RM
13'-8"x11'

SECOND FLOOR

Rustic Luxury

Features

- Large first-floor office or den.
- Mud room and lavatory off garage.
- Family room with fireplace.
- Formal and informal dining areas.
- Three large bedrooms plus master bedroom on second floor.
- Three lavatories plus tub room on second floor.

First Floor	1,560 sq. ft.
Second Floor	1,200 sq. ft.
Total Living Area	2,760 sq. ft.

PRICE CODE: C

CUSTOMIZE IT!

ORDER TOLL FREE 1■800■533■4350   24-HOUR FAX ORDERING 1■800■344■4293

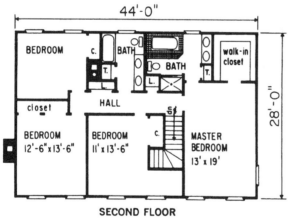

44'-0"

BEDROOM

c.

BATH

BATH

walk-in closet

28'-0"

closet

HALL

BEDROOM
12'-6" x 13'-6"

BEDROOM
11' x 13'-6"

c.

MASTER BEDROOM
13' x 19'

SECOND FLOOR

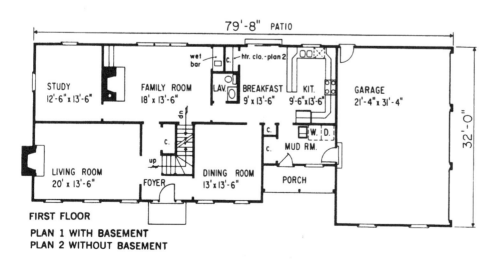

79'-8"   PATIO

STUDY
12'-6" x 13'-6"

FAMILY ROOM
18' x 13'-6"

wet bar

c.

htr. clo. - plan 2

LAV.

BREAKFAST
9' x 13'-6"

KIT.
9'-6" x 13'-6"

GARAGE
21'-4" x 31'-4"

32'-0"

LIVING ROOM
20' x 13'-6"

FOYER

up

DINING ROOM
13' x 13'-6"

c.

W. D.

c.

MUD RM.

PORCH

FIRST FLOOR

PLAN 1 WITH BASEMENT
PLAN 2 WITHOUT BASEMENT

Colonial Bourne

Features

- Elegance and versatility in a classic, Colonial design.
- Two entrances grace the front of this home, a formal foyer and a porch entrance to the mud room.
- Large living room with fireplace.
- Family room with fireplace.
- Secluded study for work or relaxation.
- Upstairs, three bedrooms share a full bath with double vanity.
- Master bedroom with large walk-in closet and private bath/shower.
- Executive three-car garage.

First Floor	1,531 sq. ft.
Second Floor	1,232 sq. ft.
Total Living Area	2,763 sq. ft.

PRICE CODE: C

Second Floor

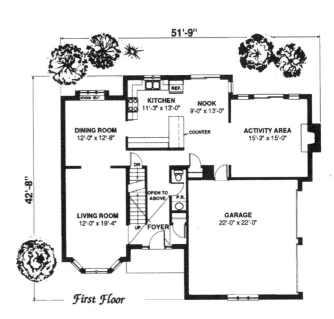

First Floor

Southern Charm

Features

- Dramatic roof lines and brick exterior make this design a stand-out.
- Cheerful entrance foyer features an open ceiling and accent windows.
- Spacious kitchen with breakfast nook.
- Activity area with fireplace.

- Large master bedroom upstairs with vaulted ceilings, separate dressing area, ample his/her closets, and deluxe master bath with private toilet.
- Three additional bedrooms upstairs share a full bath.

First Floor	1,245 sq. ft.
Second Floor	1,828 sq. ft.
Total Living Area	3,073 sq. ft.

PRICE CODE: C

CUSTOMIZE IT!

ORDER TOLL FREE 1▪800▪533▪4350 **24-HOUR FAX ORDERING** 1▪800▪344▪4293

PLAN SH91-2782

146

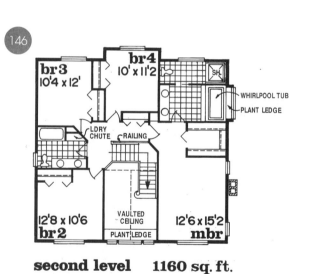

second level   1160 sq. ft.

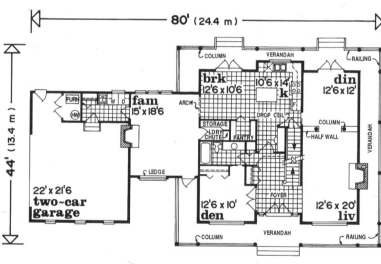

first level   1622 sq.ft.
9' CEILINGS

Features

- Grand farmhouse suits a growing family.
- Living and dining room is visually divided by half walls with decorative columns.
- Country kitchen extends to a spacious family room for informal gatherings around the fireplace.
- Master bedroom hosts a walk-in closet and divided ensuite with a whirlpool tub and twin vanity.
- Plan includes a basement and crawlspace foundation.

Total Living Area: 2,782 sq. ft.

PRICE CODE: C

PLAN FD7970-L

Attic Storage

Loft
17x10
7'-0" Clg.

Sloping Clg.
4' Half Wall

DN
UP

Bonus Room
30x17
8'-0" Clg.

Sloping Clg.   Sloping Clg.

← 101'-0" →

Covered Patio

Covered Veranda

FamilyRm
16x20

Walk-In Closet

MstrBed
18x14
Vaulted Clg. Rm.

LivRm
17x16

Brkfst
12x10

Pwdr

3-Car Gar
24x32
8'-0" Clg.

Bed#2
13x11

Gallery

Kit
17x14

© Copyright Fillmore Design Group

58'-8"

Bed#3
14x11

Utit

Bed#4/
Study
12x13

Ent

FmlDin
12x13

Shop Area
8'-0" Clg.

Covered Porch

Total Living Area   2,787 sq. ft.

PRICE CODE: C

CUSTOMIZE IT!

ORDER TOLL FREE   1■800■533■4350   24-HOUR FAX ORDERING   1■800■344■4293

148

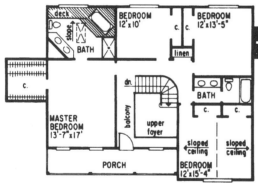

SECOND FLOOR

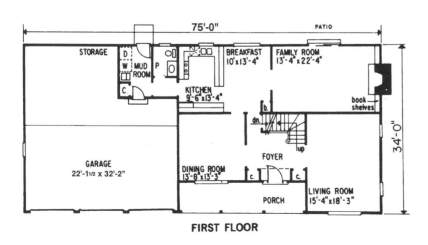

FIRST FLOOR

Country Remembrance

Features

- Functional porches on both floors of this home add distinction and warmth.
- Central, two-story foyer leads to living room on the right and the dining room on the left.
- A 22-foot long family room with fireplace opens onto the rear patio.
- Country-sized kitchen has adjacent breakfast area.
- Master bedroom with walk-in closet includes a deluxe bath with corner platform tub, angled vanity, and separate shower.
- Front bedroom features a vaulted ceiling and half-circle window.
- Additional bedrooms and full bath upstairs.

First Floor	1,428 sq. ft.
Second Floor	1,369 sq. ft.
Total Living Area	2,797 sq. ft.

PRICE CODE: C

CUSTOMIZE IT!

ORDER TOLL FREE **1▪800▪533▪4350**   24-HOUR FAX ORDERING **1▪800▪344▪4293**

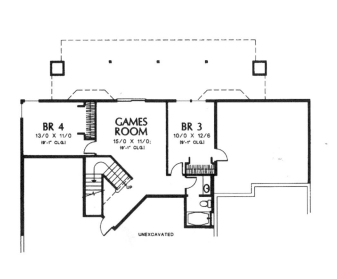

BR 4
13/0 X 11/0
(9'-1" CLG.)

GAMES ROOM
15/0 X 11/0;
(9'-1" CLG.)

BR 3
10/0 X 12/6
(9'-1" CLG.)

UP

UNEXCAVATED

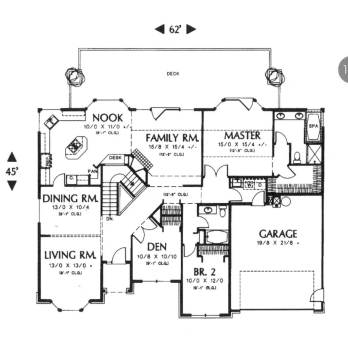

◀ 62' ▶

DECK

NOOK
10/0 X 11/0 +/-
(9'-1" CLG.)

FAMILY RM.
15/8 X 15/4 +/-
(12'-5" CLG.)

MASTER
15/0 X 15/4 +/-
(12'-5" CLG.)

SPA

45'

DESK
PAN.

DINING RM.
13/0 X 10/4
(9'-1" CLG.)

(12'-6" CLG.)

DN.

W

LIVING RM.
13/0 X 13/0 +
(9'-1" CLG.)

DEN
10/8 X 10/10
(9'-1" CLG.)

BR. 2
10/0 X 12/0
(9'-1" CLG.)

GARAGE
19/8 X 21/8 +

Lower Floor	837 sq. ft.
First Floor	1,972 sq. ft.
Total Living Area	2,809 sq. ft

PRICE CODE: C

CUSTOMIZE IT!

ORDER TOLL FREE   1▪800▪533▪4350   24-HOUR FAX ORDERING   1▪800▪344▪4293

150

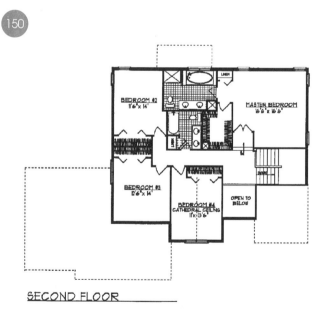

SECOND FLOOR

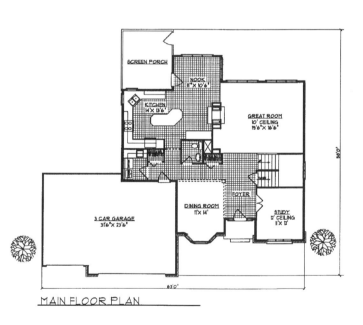

MAIN FLOOR PLAN

First Floor	1,515 sq. ft.
Second Floor	1,294 sq. ft.
Total Living Area	2,809 sq. ft.

PRICE CODE: C

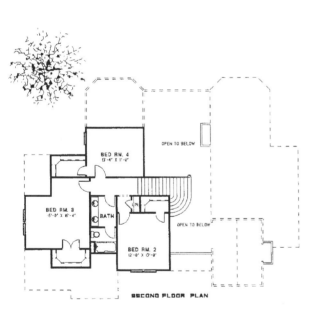

SECOND FLOOR PLAN

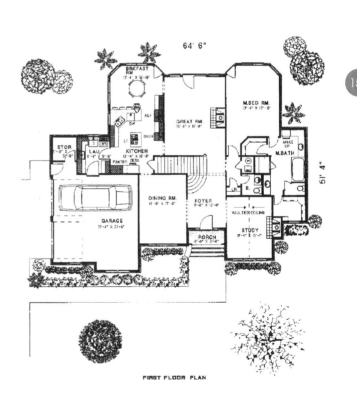

FIRST FLOOR PLAN

151

First Floor	2,002 sq. ft.
Second Floor	843 sq. ft.
Total Living Area	2,845 sq. ft.

PRICE CODE: C

PLAN DB1486

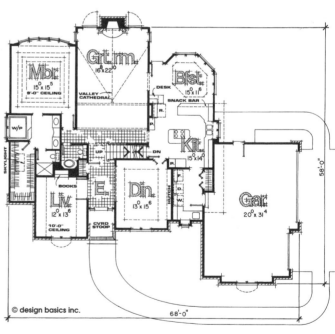

© design basics inc.

Features

- Tall entry, arched windows and brick details create a beautiful elevation.
- 2-story entry with impressive transom window has views to formal living room, dining room and large great room.
- Formal dining room features hutch space.
- Spacious great room has valley cathedral ceiling and fireplace framed by windows.
- Luxurious master suite with bowed window

and tiered ceiling.
- Master bath includes whirlpool, his and her vanity, large skylit walk-in closet and compartmented stool and shower.
- Elegant second level bridge overlooks great room and entry.
- Private 3/4 bath off fourth bedroom.

First Floor	1,972 sq. ft.
Second Floor	893 sq. ft.
Total Living Area	2,865 sq. ft.

PRICE CODE: D

CUSTOMIZE IT!

ORDER TOLL FREE 1■800■533■4350   24-HOUR FAX ORDERING 1■800■344■4293

PLAN AM2278

BR. 2
12/0 X 12/4

BONUS RM.
15/8 X 15/2

BR. 3
13/0 X 11/0

MASTER
13/6 X 16/2

FOYER
BELOW

PLANT SHELF

SPA TUB

LINEN

SKYLITE

45'

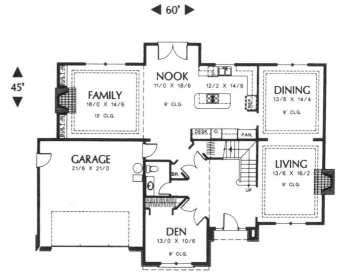

◀ 60' ▶

NOOK
11/0 X 18/6
9' CLG.

12/2 X 14/6

DINING
13/6 X 14/4
9' CLG.

FAMILY
18/0 X 14/6
13' CLG.

GARAGE
21/6 X 21/0

DESK

PAN.

LIVING
13/6 X 16/2
9' CLG.

DEN
13/0 X 10/6
9' CLG.

UP

153

First Floor	1,665 sq. ft.
Second Floor	1,202 sq. ft.
Total Living Area	2,867 sq. ft.

PRICE CODE: C

154

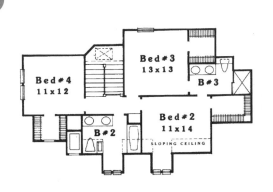

Bed #4
11x12

Bed #3
13x13

B #3

B #2

Bed #2
11x14

SLOPING CEILING

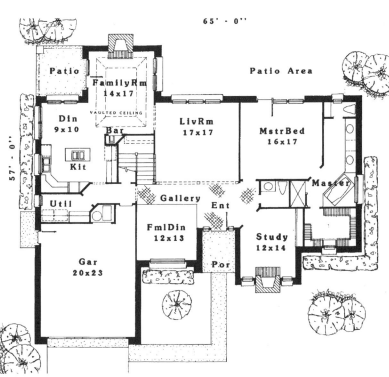

65' - 0''

57' - 0''

Patio

FamilyRm
14x17

Patio Area

Din
9x10

VAULTED CEILING

LivRm
17x17

MstrBed
16x17

Bar

Kit

Util

Gallery

Ent

Master

Gar
20x23

FmlDin
12x13

Por

Study
12x14

First Floor	2,081 sq. ft.
Second Floor	808 sq. ft.
Total Living Area	2,889 sq. ft.

PRICE CODE: C

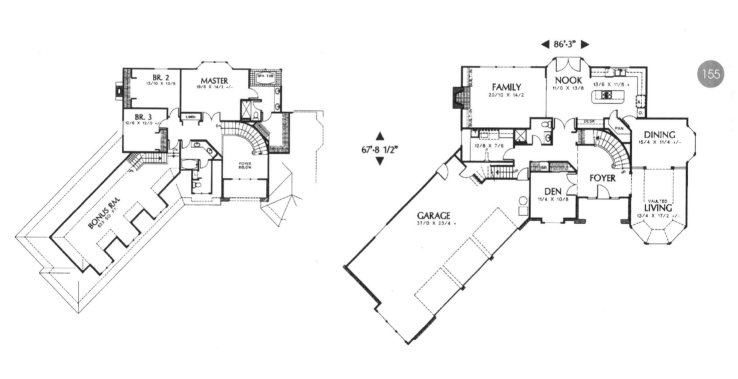

First Floor	1,758 sq. ft.
Second Floor	1,109 sq. ft.
Total Living Area	2,867 sq. ft.
Bonus Room	+623 sq. ft.

PRICE CODE: C

PLAN DB1560

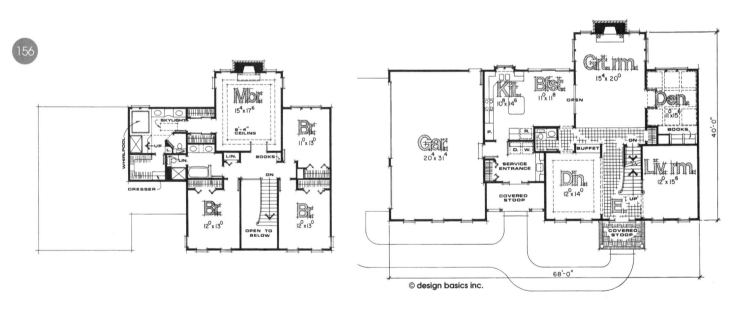

© design basics inc.

Features

- Elegant 2-story entry.
- Central hallway connects major living areas.
- Covered porch at service entry leads to mud/laundry room.
- Roomy island kitchen with built-in pantry and breakfast area.
- Fireplace in spacious master suite with 3 closets and built-in dresser.
- Sophisticated skylit master bath with 2-person whirlpool and plant shelf.
- Compartmented bath with separate tub and shower for secondary bedrooms.

First Floor	**1,536 sq. ft.**
Second Floor	**1,343 sq. ft.**
Total Living Area	**2,879 sq. ft.**

PRICE CODE: D

CUSTOMIZE IT!

ORDER TOLL FREE 1 ▪ 800 ▪ 533 ▪ 4350   **24-HOUR FAX ORDERING** 1 ▪ 800 ▪ 344 ▪ 4293

PLAN VL2888

157

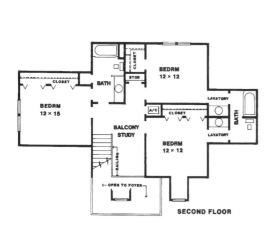

SECOND FLOOR

BEDRM 12 × 15

BATH

CLOSET

BEDRM 12 × 12

STOR

A/C **CLOSET**

LAVATORY

LAVATORY

BATH

BALCONY STUDY

BEDRM 12 × 12

RAILING

OPEN TO FOYER

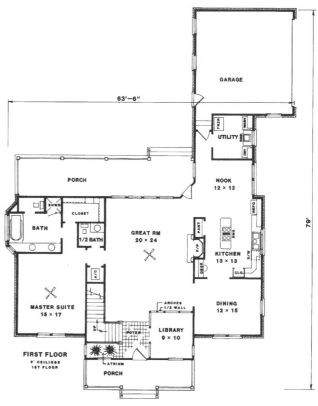

FIRST FLOOR
9' CEILINGS 1ST FLOOR

GARAGE

63'–6"

79'

UTILITY — FRZR, WASH, DWR

PORCH

NOOK 12 × 12

BATH — SHWR, CLOSET

1/2 BATH

GREAT RM 20 × 24

F/P **PANT**

REFR

KITCHEN 13 × 13

D/W **CLO.**

A/C

MASTER SUITE 15 × 17

ARCHES 1/2 WALL

DINING 12 × 15

FOYER

LIBRARY 9 × 10

ATRIUM

PORCH

First Floor	1,935 sq. ft.
Second Floor	953 sq. ft.
Total Living Area	2,888 sq. ft.

PRICE CODE: C

CUSTOMIZE IT!

ORDER TOLL FREE **1 ■ 800 ■ 533 ■ 4350**   24-HOUR FAX ORDERING **1 ■ 800 ■ 344 ■ 4293**

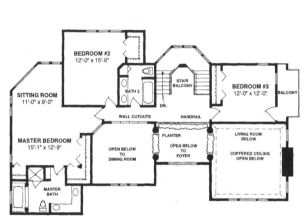

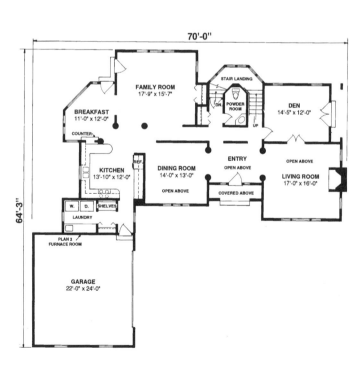

Charmaigne Estate

Features

- Unique exterior design hints at the spacious interior of this home.
- Interior features open ceilings with wrap-around staircase and full bay windows on stair landing.
- First-floor right wing contains a den and open-ceiling living room with fireplace.
- L-shaped kitchen, and separate, sunny breakfast room.
- Second floor features a large master bedroom with equally generous sitting room for quiet moments.
- Two additional upstairs bedrooms share a second full bath

First Floor	**1,866 sq. ft.**
Second Floor	**1,314 sq. ft.**
Total Living Area	**3,180 sq. ft.**

PRICE CODE: C

CUSTOMIZE IT!

ORDER TOLL FREE 1 ▪ 800 ▪ 533 ▪ 4350   **24-HOUR FAX ORDERING** 1 ▪ 800 ▪ 344 ▪ 4293

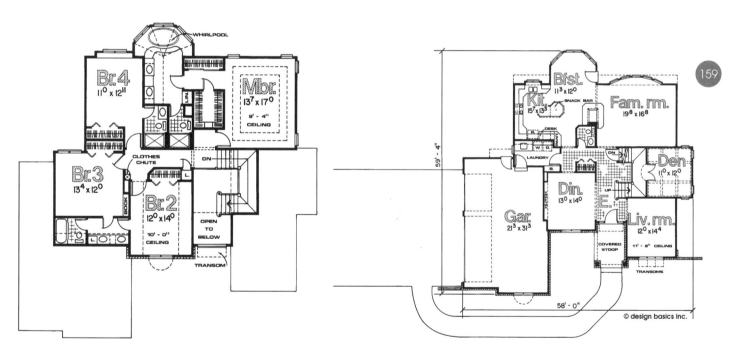

159

© design basics inc.

WHIRLPOOL

Br. 4
11⁰ x 12¹¹

Mbr.
13⁷ x 17⁰
9' - 4"
CEILING

CLOTHES CHUTE

Br. 3
13⁴ x 12⁰

Br. 2
12⁰ x 14⁰
10' - 0"
CEILING

DN.

OPEN TO BELOW

TRANSOM

Bfst.
11³ x 12⁰

Kit.
15⁷ x 13³
SNACK BAR

Fam. rm.
19⁸ x 16⁸

DESK
W. D.
LAUNDRY

Din.
13⁰ x 14⁰

DN.

Den
11⁰ x 12⁰

Gar.
21³ x 31³

Liv. rm.
12⁰ x 14⁴
11' - 8" CEILING

COVERED STOOP

TRANSOMS

59' - 4"

58' - 0"

Features

- Family room with elegant bowed windows shares showy 3-sided fireplace.
- Landing up a half-flight of stairs reveals double doors into bright den.
- Bayed dinette and island kitchen with snack bar view fireplace.

- All secondary bedrooms have access to Hollywood bath or private bath.
- Beautiful arched window for bedroom #2. Tiered ceiling in private master suite.
- Irresistible oval whirlpool tub in bayed dressing area.

First Floor	1,583 sq. ft.
Second Floor	1,331 sq. ft.
Total Living Area	2,914 sq. ft.

PRICE CODE: D

CUSTOMIZE IT!

ORDER TOLL FREE **1▪800▪533▪4350** 24-HOUR FAX ORDERING **1▪800▪344▪4293**

160

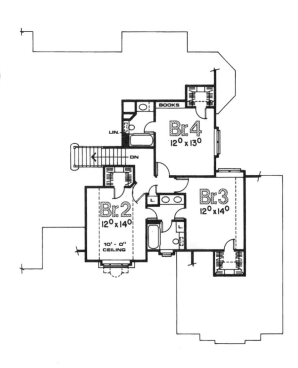

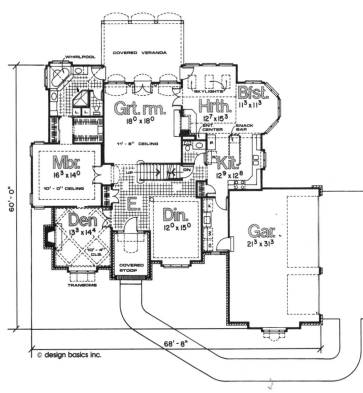

© design basics inc.

Features

- Majestic elevation with side-load garage combines stucco, brick and elegant details for instant curb appeal.
- Entry surveys great room and dining room.
- Intriguing ceiling in den with cozy fireplace.
- Open, formal dining room extends entertaining space.
- Elegant great room with see-thru fireplace and French doors to covered veranda.
- Lovely hearth room features three skylights, a wall of three large picture/awning windows and an

entertainment center.
- Sunny bayed dinette and kitchen with island, snack bar, wrapping counters and pantry enhance daily family living.
- Three secondary bedrooms upstairs, each with a walk-in closet and ample bathroom space; bedroom #4 has built-in bookcase.
- Main level sumptuous master suite affords luxury accommodations with two closets, whirlpool tub, his and her vanities and access to a covered veranda

First Floor	2,084 sq. ft.
Second Floor	848 sq. ft.
Total Living Area	2,932 sq. ft.

PRICE CODE: D

CUSTOMIZE IT!

ORDER TOLL FREE 1▪800▪533▪4350   24-HOUR FAX ORDERING 1▪800▪344▪4293

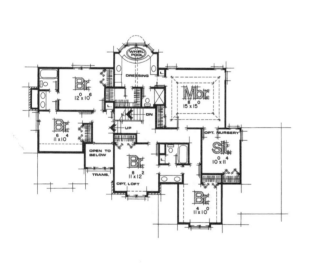

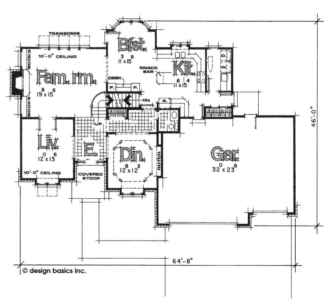

© design basics inc.

64'-8"

46'-0"

Features

- Optimized main level, maximized second level.
- Connected by French doors, family room and living room both feature 10-foot ceilings and transom windows.
- Large island kitchen includes snack bar and lazy Susan, plus large desk and pantry cabinets in bayed breakfast area.

- Second level with 5 bedrooms, 3 bathrooms and many closets.
- Master suite with French doors leading to private sitting room/nursery.
- Beautiful master bath with his and her vanities and oval whirlpool tub.

First Floor	1,349 sq. ft.
Second Floor	1,592 sq. ft.
Total Living Area	2,941 sq. ft.

PRICE CODE: D

CUSTOMIZE IT!

ORDER TOLL FREE 1■800■533■4350   **24-HOUR FAX ORDERING** 1■800■344■4293

PLAN FD8181-L

162

75'-0"

62'-5"

Covered Patio

MstrBed
15x17
Sloped Clg.
9'-0" To 12'-0"

Patio

Din
13x10
9'-0" Clg.

Bed#4
11x12
9'-0" Clg.

LivRm
13x16
9'-0" Clg.

FamilyRm
17x20
Vaulted Clg.
9'-0" To 11'-0"

Bed#3
13x11
9'-0" Clg.

Kit
13x13
9'-0" Clg.

Gallery
9'-0" Clg.

Bed#2
13x11
9'-0" Clg.

Pwdr

Ent

FmlDin
13x12
9'-0" Clg.

Util

Walk-in Closet

Study
12x11
Sloped Clg.
9'-0" To 12'-0"

Cov.
Porch

3-Car Gar
30x23
9'-4" Clg.

Total Living Area   2,945 sq. ft.

PRICE CODE: C

CUSTOMIZE IT!

ORDER TOLL FREE   1■800■533■4350   **24-HOUR FAX ORDERING**   1■800■344■4293

PLAN DB2230

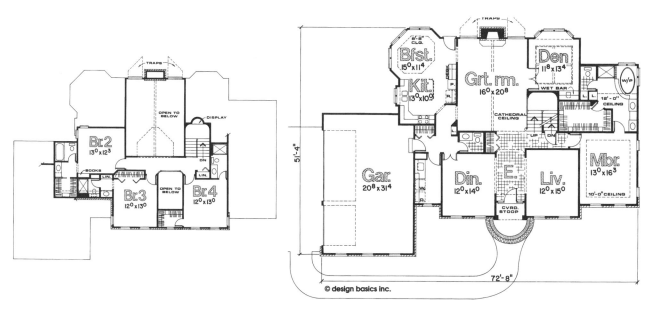

© design basics inc.

163

Features

- Elegant brick elevation and rows of shuttered windows lend timeless beauty to colonial design.
- 2-story entry hall surveys formal dining and living rooms and views magnificent great room.
- French doors lead from dining room into back hall for quick kitchen service.
- Den is comfortably secluded, yet conveniently placed next to great room and enhanced by French doors.

- Window-lit utility/laundry with soaking sink strategically tucked near garage entrance and convenient hall closet.
- Master suite has boxed ceiling and luxurious dressing/bath area with large walk-in closet, built-in dresser, his and her vanities, oval whirlpool.

First Floor	2,063 sq. ft.
Second Floor	894 sq. ft.
Total Living Area	2,957 sq. ft.

PRICE CODE: D

164

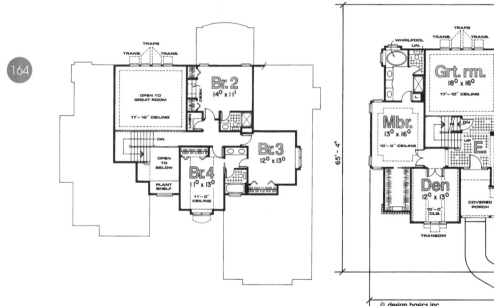

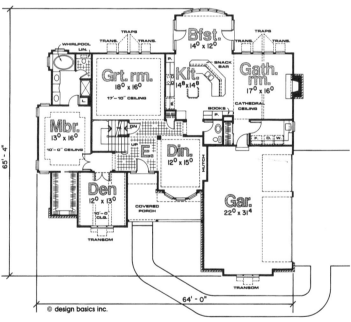

© design basics inc.

Features

- Wood-railed porch and repeating window treatment combine for traditional front elevation.
- Entry offers views to formal entertaining areas.
- 9-foot main level walls.
- Den has lovely window and 10-foot ceiling.
- Well-designed kitchen features 2 pantries and large food preparation area situated to flow into casual areas.
- Tall windows center on cathedral ceiling in

gathering room with raised hearth fireplace and bookcase.
- Master bedroom features French door entry, unique ceiling design, and spacious walk-in closet.
- Upstairs balcony overlooks great room and entry with plant shelf.
- Twin closets flank built-in desk in bedroom #2 with its own 3/4 bath.

First Floor	**2,158 sq. ft**
Second Floor	**821 sq. ft**
Total Living Area	**2,979 sq. ft**

PRICE CODE: D

PLAN NP NANTUCKET

SECOND FLOOR

BEDROOM 3
14'-3" x 13'-3"

GUEST ROOM
10'-6" x 13'-2"

CLOSET

MASTER BATH

WHIRLPOOL

WALK IN CLOSET

BATH

WALK IN CLOSET

WALK IN CLOSET

WALK IN CLOSET

LIN

W D

BEDROOM 2
14'-3" x 13'-2"

STUDY ROOM
10'-1" x 10'-2"

MASTER BEDROOM
14'-6" x 18'-2"

FIRST FLOOR

BRICK PAVED PATIO

MICROWAVE

KITCHEN

BREAKFAST

REF.

D.W.

OVEN

MUD RM

BUTLER PANTRY

PDR RM.

FAMILY ROOM
15'-6 1/2 x 16'-5"

LIVING ROOM
14'-6" x 18'-6"

DINING ROOM
15'-0" x 14'-2"

FOYER

BRICK PAVERS

Features

- This two story colonial home has everything.
- First floor features a grand foyer with stately stair case and a large formal living room, separated from the family room by pocket doors.
- 9' ceilings are throughout the house.
- The kitchen is spacious and includes a mud room,

a butler pantry and a breakfast nook with bay window.

- Second floor features a large Master Suite with a fireplace and ample closet area.
- There is a study off the Master Suite with stairs leading to the expandable attic.

First Floor	1,511 sq. ft.
Second Floor	1,511 sq. ft.
Attic	947 sq. ft.
Total Living Area	3,969 sq. ft.

PRICE CODE: E

PLAN VL3011

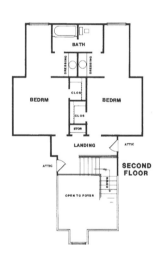

SECOND FLOOR

BATH

DRESSING · DRESSING

BEDRM · BEDRM

CLOS

CLOS

STOR

LANDING · ATTIC

ATTIC

OPEN TO FOYER

24'

WORK SHOP

2 CARS

DETACHED CARPORT

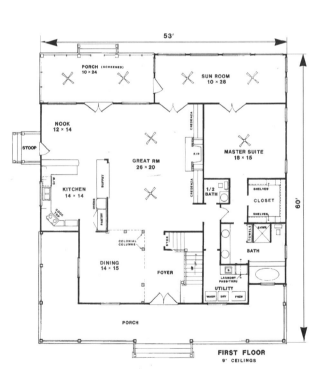

53'

PORCH (SCREENED) 10 × 24

SUN ROOM 10 × 28

NOOK 12 × 14

GREAT RM 26 × 20

MASTER SUITE 18 × 15

STOOP

KITCHEN 14 × 14

BUFFET

F/P

1/2 BATH

SHELVES

CLOSET

SHELVES

COOK TOP

OVENS

PANTRY

COLONIAL COLUMNS

STO.

BATH

60'

DINING 14 × 15

FOYER

LAUNDRY PASS-THRU

UTILITY

WASH DRY FRZR

PORCH

FIRST FLOOR
9' CEILINGS

First Floor	2,361 sq. ft.
Second Floor	650 sq. ft.
Total Living Area	3,011 sq. ft.

PRICE CODE: C

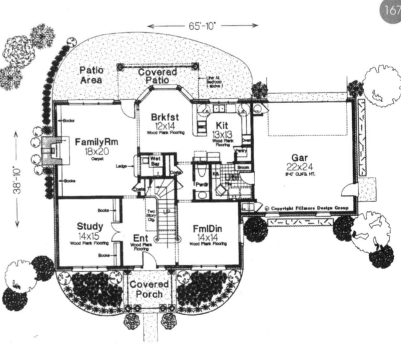

First Floor 1,573 sq. ft.
Second Floor 1,449 sq. ft.
Total Living Area 3,022 sq. ft.

PRICE CODE: C

PLAN DB987

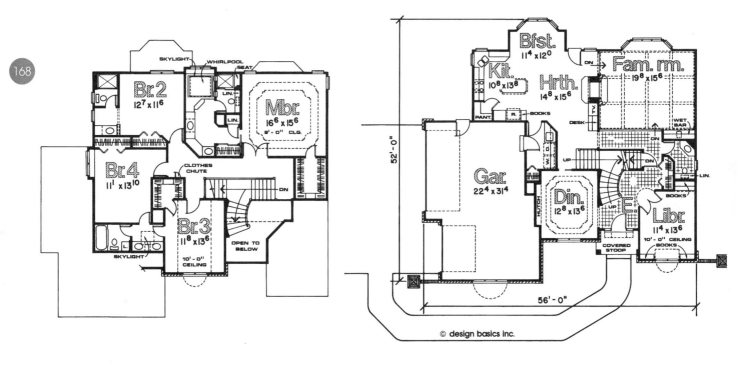

© design basics inc.

Features

- Volume entry with curving staircase views dining room with gorgeous ceiling detail and hutch space.
- Sunken family room with spider-beamed ceiling, bayed window, wet bar and see-thru fireplace.
- Island kitchen adjoins bayed breakfast area and hearth room with fireplace, entertainment center and built-in desk.

- Elegant master suite with special ceiling detail includes his and her closets, wrapping vanity and 2-person whirlpool.
- Third bedroom offering walk-in closet shares skylit bath with fourth bedroom

First Floor	1,583 sq. ft.
Second Floor	1,442 sq. ft.
Total Living Area	3,025 sq. ft.

PRICE CODE: D

169

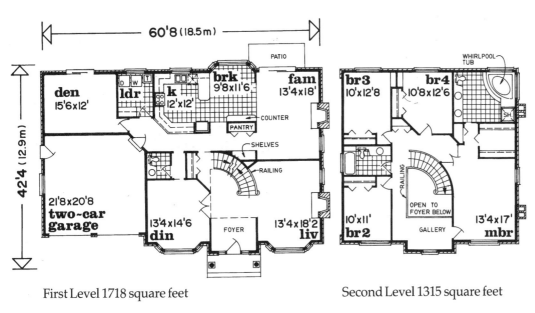

First Level 1718 square feet

Second Level 1315 square feet

Features

- Kitchen, with pantry and abundant counter space, is open to the breakfast bay and family room.
- Sliding glass access to the patio and fireplace makes the family room an ideal gathering spot.
- Game room can easily be used as an office, studio or guest room.
- Bay windows adorn the living and dining rooms.
- Curved staircase ascends to a railed gallery and library which views the foyer below.
- Master bedroom features a walk-in wardrobe and lavish ensuite with twin vanity and whirlpool spa.
- Library, which opens to the master bedroom, is an ideal computer station.

Total Living Area   3,033 sq. ft.

PRICE CODE: C

CUSTOMIZE IT!

ORDER TOLL FREE   1■800■533■4350   24-HOUR FAX ORDERING   1■800■344■4293

PLAN DB940

170

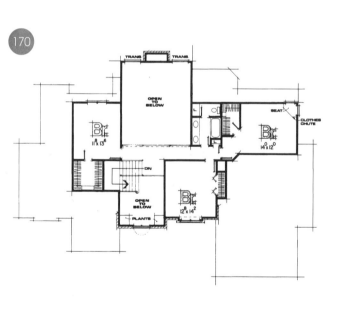

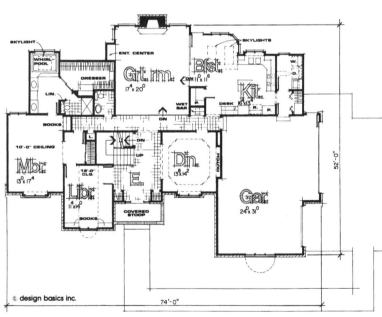

© design basics inc.

74'-0"

52'-0"

Features

- 2-story-high entry with plant shelves atop dual coat closets.
- Wet bar convenient to dining room with hutch space.
- French doors open into library with volume ceiling and built-in bookcases .
- Sunken great room with sloped ceiling and built-in entertainment center spotlights beautiful fireplace .

- Master bedroom with built-in bookcase adjoins skylit bath area with double vanity, large walk-in closet with mirrored bypass doors plus built-in ,dresser and 2-person whirlpool tub.
- Secondary bedrooms share hall bath.

First Floor	2,078 sq. ft.
Second Floor	960 sq. ft.
Total Living Area	3,038 sq. ft.

PRICE CODE: D

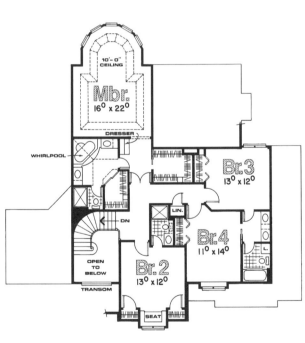

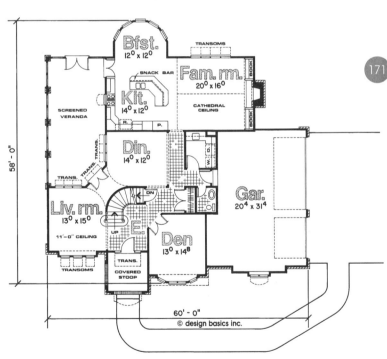

171

Features

- Stucco accents and graceful window treatments enhance front elevation.
- French doors open to large screened-in veranda ideal for outdoor entertaining.
- Open living room and handsome curved staircase add drama to entry area.
- Gourmet kitchen, spacious bayed dinette and volume family room flow together for easy living.
- Elegant bayed master bedroom with 10 foot vaulted ceiling is situated to the back of the home for privacy.
- 2 walk-in closets, his and her lavs, corner whirlpool and compartmented shower and stool highlight dressing area

First Floor	1,631 sq. ft.
Second Floor	1,426 sq. ft.
Total Living Area	3,057 sq. ft.

PRICE CODE: D

PLAN NP1212

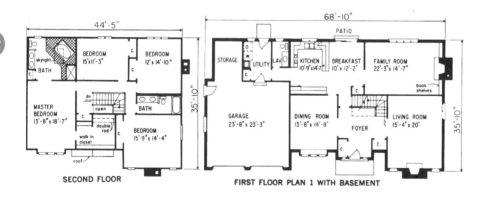

SECOND FLOOR

FIRST FLOOR PLAN 1 WITH BASEMENT

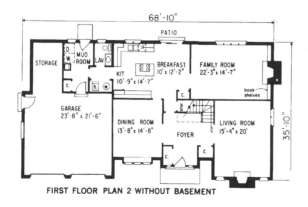

FIRST FLOOR PLAN 2 WITHOUT BASEMENT

Hearthstone

Features

- Full-length windows rising two-stories give this home a lofty look.
- Elegant front entrance with double-sided windows lead to foyer.
- Foyer fronts open, winding staircase.
- Right wing includes front living room with fireplace and rear family room with fireplace.
- Left wing contains dining room with entrance to breakfast room adjacent to kitchen with center cooking island.
- Upstairs, the left wing contains the master bedroom suite, with master bath with separate shower, step-up tub and skylight.
- Three additional bedrooms share a full bath.

First Floor	1,644 sq. ft.
Second Floor	1,458 sq. ft.
Total Living Area	3,102 sq. ft.

PRICE CODE: C

PLAN MN3101

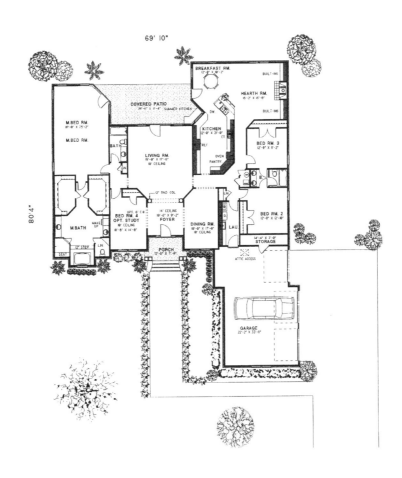

173

Total Living Area **3,101 sq. ft.**

PRICE CODE: C

PLAN NP1223

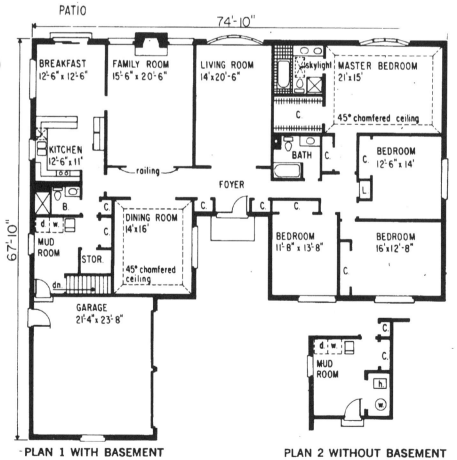

PATIO

74'-10"

BREAKFAST
12'-6" x 12'-6"

FAMILY ROOM
15'-6" x 20'-6"

LIVING ROOM
14'x20'-6"

skylight

MASTER BEDROOM
21'x15'

45° chamfered ceiling

KITCHEN
12'-6" x 11'

railing

FOYER

C.

BATH

C.

BEDROOM
12'-6" x 14'

B.

d w.

MUD ROOM

C.

DINING ROOM
14'x16'

C.

C.

C.

BEDROOM
11'-8" x 13'-8"

BEDROOM
16'x12'-8"

STOR.

45° chamfered ceiling

C.

dn.

67'-10"

GARAGE
21'-4" x 23'-8"

d w.

C.

C.

MUD ROOM

h.

w.

PLAN 1 WITH BASEMENT

PLAN 2 WITHOUT BASEMENT

French Individualist

Features

- This handsome home shows off its French styling, highlighted with brick, multi-panel windows, bay windows, and high-pitched roof.
- Elegant central foyer opens to reveal living quarters to the left and sleeping quarters to the right.
- Family room features a wood-burning fireplace.
- Chamfered ceilings in the dining room and master bedroom highlight unique design.
- Master bedroom suite include full bath with skylight accent.
- Three additional bedrooms share another full bath.

Total Living Area   3,108 sq. ft.

PRICE CODE: C

PLAN AM2301

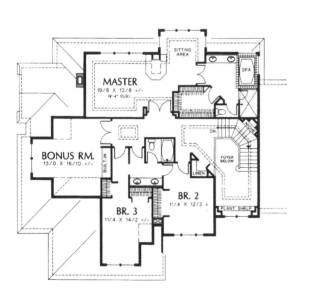

MASTER
19/8 X 13/8 +/-
(9'-4" CLG.)

SITTING AREA

SPA

BONUS RM.
13/0 X 16/10 +/-

DN.

FOYER BELOW

LINEN

BR. 2
11/4 X 12/2

BR. 3
11/4 X 14/2 +/-

PLANT SHELF

◄ 68' ►

OFFICE
11/6 X 14/6
(10'-8" CLG.)

FAMILY
18/6 X 15/8

NOOK
10/0 X 16/8 +/-
(9' CLG.)

REF.

DESK BUILT-IN

12/0 X 15/8

DINING
13/6 X 11/0
(13'-8" CLG.)

PANTRY

GARAGE
21/8 X 19/2

D.W.

BUILT-IN

UP

LIVING
13/6 X 15/0
(13'-6" CLG.)

LIBRARY
11/8 X 10/4 +/-

24/0 X 12/4

▲
53'-6"
▼

First Floor	1,779 sq. ft.
Second Floor	1,335 sq. ft.
Total Living Area	3,114 sq. ft.
Office	+209 sq. ft.
Bonus Room	+270 sq. ft.

PRICE CODE: C

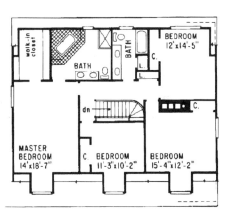

SECOND FLOOR

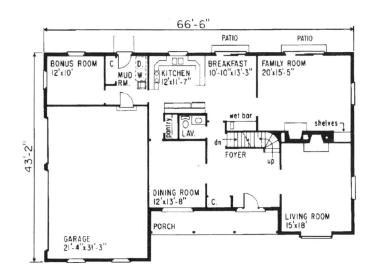

Country Tudor

Features

- Traditional styling suited to country or urban living.
- Attractive steep gable roof with dormers.
- Brick veneer with trim.
- Large foyer opens to gently curved staircase.
- Adjoining breakfast area with wet bar faces back

yard patio.
- Family room with fireplace and built-in bookcases also opens to backyard patio.
- Three large bedrooms upstairs share a full bath.
- Master bedroom suite includes a walk-in closet and deluxe bath/shower.

First Floor	1,731 sq. ft.
Second Floor	1,386 sq. ft.
Total Living Area	3,117 sq. ft.

PRICE CODE: C

CUSTOMIZE IT!

ORDER TOLL FREE 1■800■533■4350   24-HOUR FAX ORDERING   1■800■344■4293

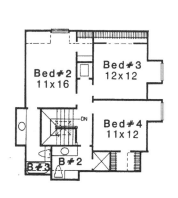

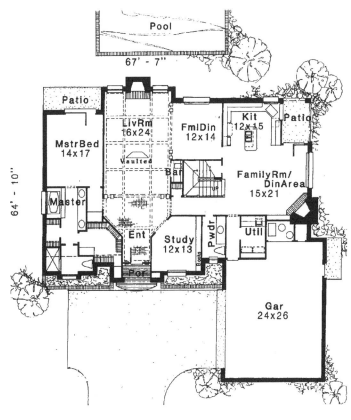

First Floor	2,283 sq. ft.
Second Floor	855 sq. ft.
Total Living Area	3,138 sq. ft.

PRICE CODE: C

HOLZHAUER INK. 93

178

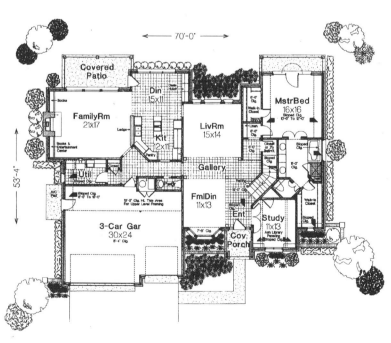

First Floor		2,237 sq. ft.
Second Floor		907 sq. ft.
Total Living Area		3,144 sq. ft.

PRICE CODE: C

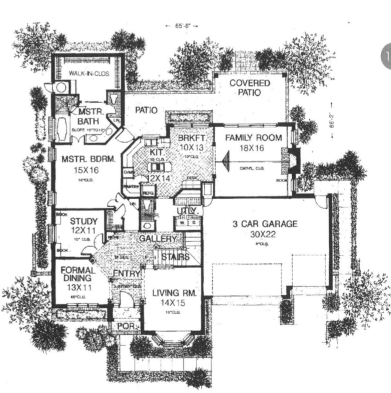

179

First Floor	2,182 sq. ft.
Second Floor	968 sq. ft.
Total Living Area	3,150 sq. ft.

PRICE CODE: C

CUSTOMIZE IT!

ORDER TOLL FREE   1■800■533■4350   24-HOUR FAX ORDERING   1■800■344■4293

PLAN FD7956-L

180

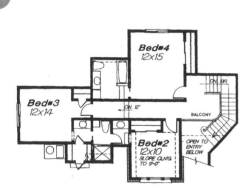

First Floor	2,243 sq. ft.
Second Floor	908 sq. ft.
Total Living Area	3,151 sq. ft.

PRICE CODE: C

181

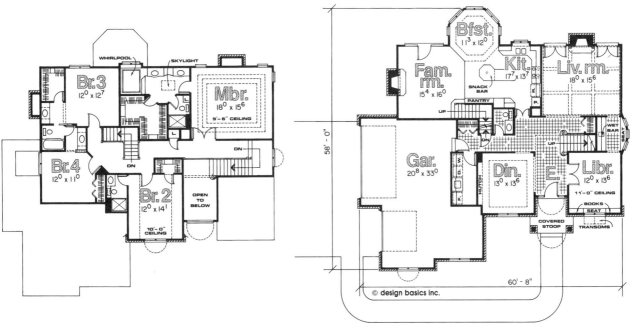

© design basics inc.

58' - 0"

60' - 8"

Features

- Inviting volume entry.
- Formal living room showcases a fireplace and spider-beamed ceiling.
- Family kitchen area with 2 pantries focuses on back yard view.
- Gourmet island kitchen with snack bar adjoins gazebo dinette.

- Generous closets and baths for roomy secondary bedrooms.
- Double doors lead into master suite with tiered ceiling and dressing/bath area including double vanity, walk-in closet and 2-person whirlpool.

First Floor	1,744 sq. ft.
Second Floor	1,474 sq. ft.
Total Living Area	3,218 sq. ft.

PRICE CODE: E

PLAN FD8227-L

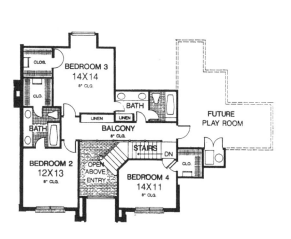

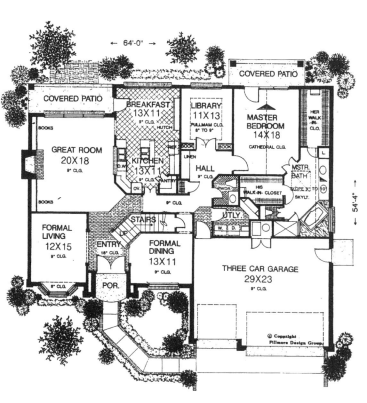

First Floor	2,236 sq. ft.
Second Floor	983 sq. ft.
Total Living Area	3,219 sq. ft.

PRICE CODE: D

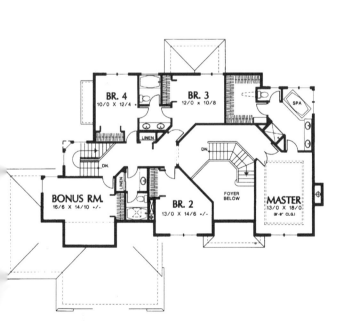

BR. 4
10/0 X 12/4

BR. 3
12/0 x 10/8

SPA

LINEN

DN.

DN.

DN.

BONUS RM.
15/6 X 14/10 +/-

LINEN

BR. 2
13/0 X 14/6 +/-

FOYER
BELOW

MASTER
13/0 X 18/0
(9'-8" CLG.)

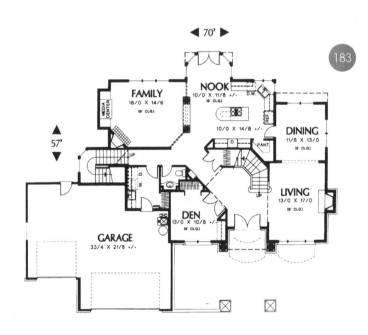

◀ 70' ▶

FAMILY
18/0 X 14/6
(9' CLG.)

NOOK
10/0 X 11/8 +/-
(9' CLG.)

D.W.

MEDIA
CENTER

10/0 X 14/8 +/-

REF.

DINING
11/6 X 13/0
(9' CLG.)

57'

UP

PANT.

W. D.

LIVING
13/0 X 17/0
(9' CLG.)

DEN
13/0 X 10/8 +/-
(9' CLG.)

UP

GARAGE
33/4 X 21/8 +/-

First Floor	1,763 sq. ft.
Second Floor	1,469 sq. ft.
Total Living Area	3,232 sq. ft.
Bonus Room	+256 sq. ft.

PRICE CODE: D

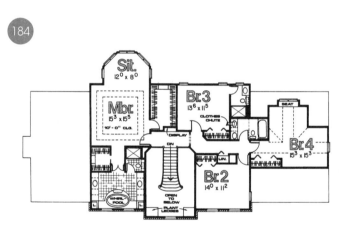

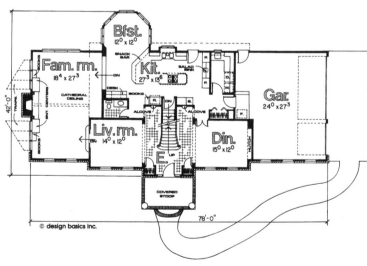

© design basics inc.

Features

- Beautiful Southern Colonial style elevation highlighted by stately columns.
- Open entry views formal areas and tapering staircase.
- 9-foot main level walls.
- Formal dining room has hutch space with access to kitchen area through double doors.
- Living room accesses family room through

attractive 10 lite pocket doors.
- Gourmet kitchen features island cooktop, snack bar, salad sink, 2 pantries, broom closet, bookcase and planning desk.
- 3-car side-load garage.
- Secondary bedrooms have 2 bath areas.
- Private master suite with tiered ceiling, 2 walk-in closets, and roomy bayed sitting area.

First Floor	1,717 sq. f
Second Floor	1,518 sq. f
Total Living Area	3,235 sq. f

PRICE CODE: E

PLAN FD7507

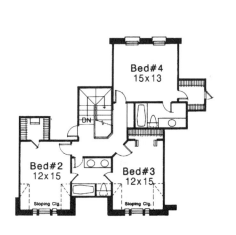

Bed#4
15x13

DN

Bed#2
12x15

Bed#3
12x15

Sloping Clg.   Sloping Clg.

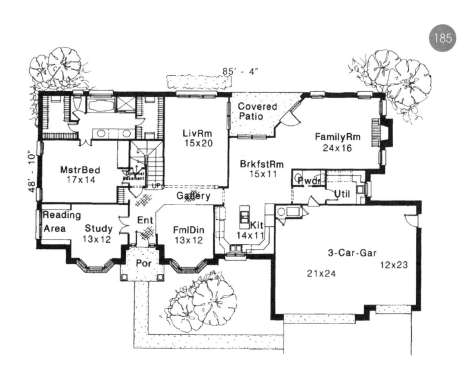

85' - 4"

48' - 10"

MstrBed
17x14

LivRm
15x20

Covered
Patio

FamilyRm
24x16

Optional
Basement

UP

BrkfstRm
15x11

Pwdr

Util

Gallery

Reading
Area

Study
13x12

Ent

FmlDin
13x12

Kit
14x11

Por

3-Car-Gar
21x24   12x23

First Floor	2,365 sq. ft.
Second Floor	874 sq. ft.
Total Living Area	3,239 sq. ft.

PRICE CODE: D

CUSTOMIZE IT!

ORDER TOLL FREE   1■800■533■4350   24-HOUR FAX ORDERING   1■800■344■4293

186

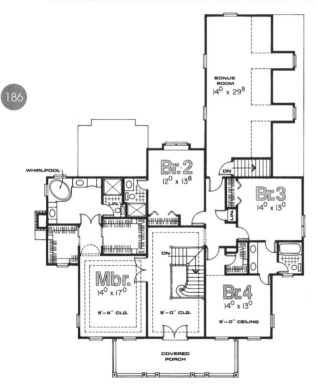

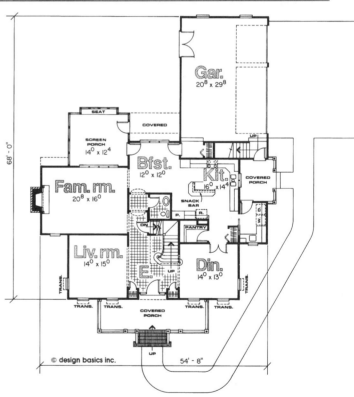

© design basics inc.

Features

- Main and second level covered porches accompanied by intricate detailing and illuminating transom windows create a splendid Southern mansion appeal.
- Prominent entry open to formal dining and living rooms.
- Roomy breakfast area provides access to screen porch and 3-car garage.

- Spacious island kitchen features snack bar, lazy Susan and access to walk-in pantry. Efficient laundry is located near kitchen with entry to small covered side porch.
- Stairs in garage lead to bonus room on second level. Huge bonus room over garage perfect for kids and storage.
- 9-foot main level walls.

First Floor	1,598 sq. ft
Second Floor	1,675 sq. ft
Total Living Area	3,273 sq. ft

PRICE CODE: E

PLAN MN3222

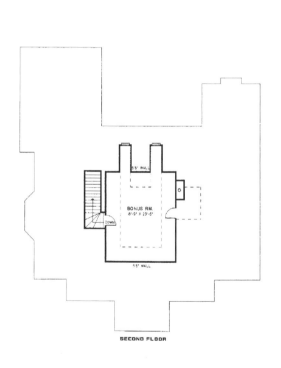

SECOND FLOOR

FIRST FLOOR

First Floor	2,768 sq. ft.
Second Floor	529 sq. ft.
Total Living Area	3,297 sq. ft.

PRICE CODE: D

188

MASTER
15/0 X 17/0

BR. 2
11/0 X 12/0

BR. 3
11/0 X 12/0

BR. 4
11/0 X 12/0
(9" CLG)

SPA TUB

DN.

LINEN

BR. 5
12/8 X 12/6

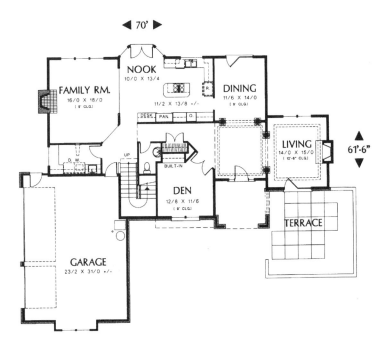

◀ 70' ▶

FAMILY RM.
16/0 X 18/0
(9" CLG)

NOOK
10/0 X 13/4

11/2 X 13/8 +/-

DINING
11/6 X 14/0
(9' CLG)

DESK   PAN.

D.W.

UP

BUILT-IN

DEN
12/8 X 11/6
(9' CLG)

LIVING
14/0 X 15/0
(12'-6" CLG)

61'-6" ▲▼

TERRACE

GARAGE
23/2 X 31/0 +/-

First Floor	1,750 sq. ft.
Second Floor	1,550 sq. ft.
Total Living Area	3,300 sq. ft.

PRICE CODE: D

CUSTOMIZE IT!

ORDER TOLL FREE   1■800■533■4350   24-HOUR FAX ORDERING   1■800■344■4293

189

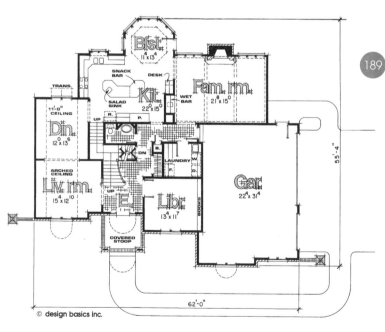

© design basics inc.

Features

- Repetitive peaks on gracious front facade.
- 9-foot main level walls.
- Extra wide hallways.
- Living room and dining room combine for formal entertaining.
- Interesting T-shaped staircase.
- Gourmet kitchen with salad sink and snack bar in island.

- Main level laundry and freezer space.
- 3-car side-load garage.
- Master suite with 2 walk-in closets and private gazebo sitting area.
- Skylit master bath offers whirlpool, double lavs and built-in dresser.
- Hollywood bath for 2 bedrooms.
- Private 3/4 bath for guest bedroom.

First Floor	1,709 sq. ft.
Second Floor	1,597 sq. ft.
Total Living Area	3,306 sq. ft.

PRICE CODE: E

CUSTOMIZE IT!

ORDER TOLL FREE 1■800■533■4350   24-HOUR FAX ORDERING 1■800■344■4293

PLAN DB1068

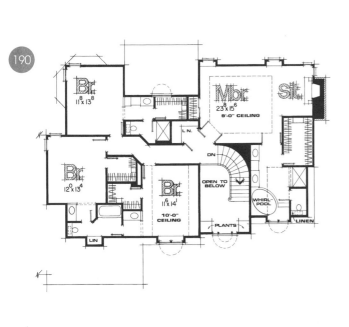

190

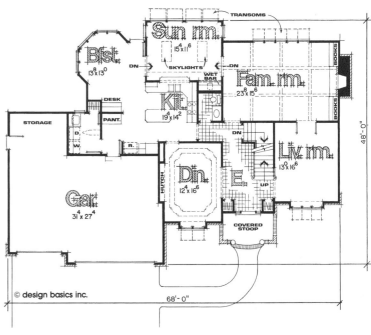

© design basics inc.

68'-0"

48'-0"

Features

- Dramatic arched covered entry and exquisite window detailing highlights elevation.
- Elegant volume entry with curving staircase flanked by formal entertaining rooms.
- Window-lit laundry has iron-a-way and handy soaking sink.
- Dining room features decorative ceiling and hutch space.
- Expansive family room has wall of transom windows and warm fireplace flanked by bookcases.
- Nearby kitchen and bayed breakfast area offers planning desk, large pantry, island and snack bar service to sun room.

First Floor	1,733 sq. ft.
Second Floor	1,586 sq. ft.
Total Living Area	3,319 sq. ft.

PRICE CODE: E

CUSTOMIZE IT!

ORDER TOLL FREE 1■800■533■4350   24-HOUR FAX ORDERING 1■800■344■4293

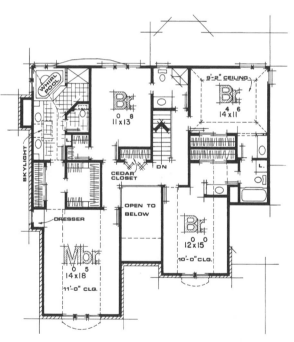

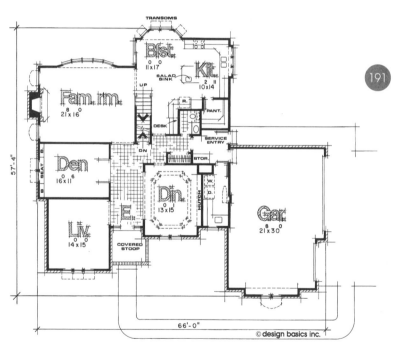

© design basics inc.

Features

- Stately elevation alludes to sophisticated living within.
- Dining room features lovely ceiling detail and large hutch space.
- French doors open to den with window seat centered between two bookcases.
- Family room boasts bowed window and arched

- transoms on each side of fireplace.
- Tall windows in bayed breakfast area.
- Master suite offers built-in dresser, his and her closets, skylight in bath, and glass block between shower and whirlpool.

First Floor	1,836 sq. ft.
Second Floor	1,501 sq. ft.
Total Living Area	3,337 sq. ft.

PRICE CODE: E

CUSTOMIZE IT!

ORDER TOLL FREE 1 ▪ 800 ▪ 533 ▪ 4350   **24-HOUR FAX ORDERING** 1 ▪ 800 ▪ 344 ▪ 4293

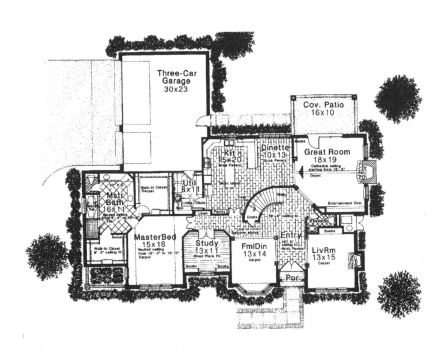

First Floor	2,437 sq. ft.
Second Floor	922 sq. ft.
Total Living Area	3,359 sq. ft.

PRICE CODE: D

PLAN·CD9101

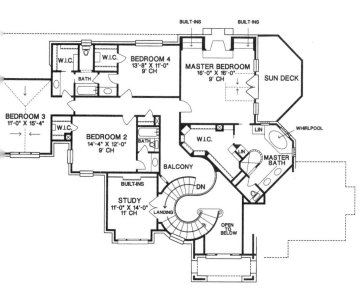

Second floor plan labels:
BUILT-INS · BUILT-INS
W.I.C. · W.I.C.
BEDROOM 4 13'-8" X 11'-0" 9' CH
MASTER BEDROOM 16'-0" X 16'-0" 9' CH
SUN DECK
BATH
BEDROOM 3 11'-0" X 15'-4"
W.I.C.
BEDROOM 2 14'-4" X 12'-0" 9' CH
BATH
LIN
W.I.C.
LIN
WHIRLPOOL
BALCONY
MASTER BATH
BUILT-INS
STUDY 11'-0" X 14'-0" 11' CH
LANDING
DN
OPEN TO BELOW

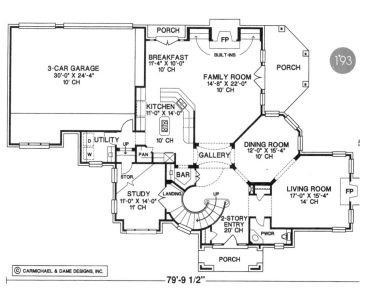

First floor plan labels:
PORCH
FP
BUILT-INS
3-CAR GARAGE 30'-0" X 24'-4" 10' CH
BREAKFAST 11'-4" X 10'-0" 10' CH
FAMILY ROOM 14'-8" X 22'-0" 10' CH
PORCH
193
KITCHEN 11'-4" X 14'-0" 10' CH
UTILITY
D
W
UP
PAN
STOR.
BAR
GALLERY
DINING ROOM 12'-0" X 15'-4" 10' CH
STUDY 11'-0" X 14'-0" 11' CH
LANDING
UP
2-STORY ENTRY 20' CH
LIVING ROOM 17'-0" X 15'-4" 14' CH
FP
PWDR
PORCH
© CARMICHAEL & DAME DESIGNS, INC.
79'-9 1/2"

BAR
UNFINISHED STORAGE BELOW STUDY
DOWN TO BASEMENT
UP

OPTIONAL BASEMENT ACCESS

First floor	1,786 sq. ft.
Second Floor	1,607 sq. ft.
Total Living Area	3,393 sq. ft.

PRICE CODE: F

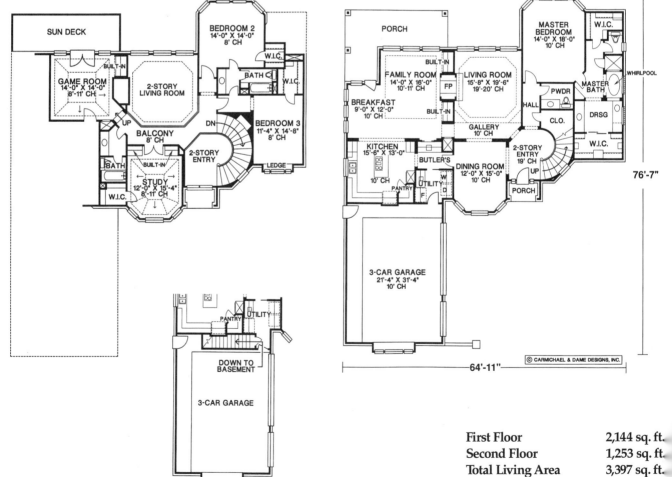

SUN DECK

GAME ROOM
14'-0" X 14'-0"
8'-11' CH →

2-STORY
LIVING ROOM

BEDROOM 2
14'-0" X 14'-0"
8' CH

W.I.C.

BATH

W.I.C.

BALCONY
8' CH

UP

DN

BEDROOM 3
11'-4" X 14'-8"
8' CH

2-STORY
ENTRY

LEDGE

BATH

BUILT-IN

STUDY
12'-0" X 15'-4"
8'-11" CH

W.I.C.

PANTRY   UTILITY

DOWN TO
BASEMENT

3-CAR GARAGE

PORCH

FAMILY ROOM
14'-0" X 16'-0"
10'-11" CH

BUILT-IN

FP

BUILT-IN

LIVING ROOM
15'-8" X 19'-6"
19'-20' CH

MASTER
BEDROOM
14'-0" X 18'-0"
10' CH

W.I.C.

BREAKFAST
9'-0" X 12'-0"
10' CH

PWDR

MASTER
BATH

WHIRLPOOL

GALLERY
10' CH

HALL

CLO.

DRSG

KITCHEN
15'-6" X 13'-0"
10' CH

BUTLER'S

DINING ROOM
12'-0" X 15'-0"
10' CH

2-STORY
ENTRY
19' CH

W.I.C.

PANTRY

UTILITY
W
D
F

UP

PORCH

76'-7"

3-CAR GARAGE
21'-4" X 31'-4"
10' CH

64'-11"

© CARMICHAEL & DAME DESIGNS, INC.

First Floor	2,144 sq. ft.
Second Floor	1,253 sq. ft.
Total Living Area	3,397 sq. ft.

PRICE CODE: F

PLAN DB3174

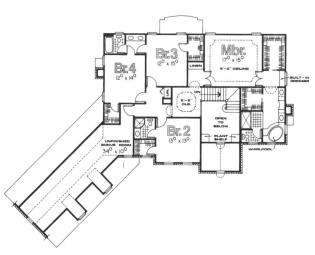

195

Features

- Gabled roofs, numerous windows and angled garage accent this magnificent elevation.
- 2-story entry opens to formal living room with fireplace and transom windows.
- Private den has spider-beamed ceiling accents and transom windows.
- Breakfast area, highlighted by a bowed window, features a desk and 2 pantries.

- Grand family room with ceiling accents and fireplace is located close to large laundry room and 3-car garage.
- Bedroom #2 has private 3/4 bath featuring corner shower.
- Master suite offers 2 walk-in closets, built-in dresser, dual lavs, whirlpool bath and open shower.
- Bedrooms #3 and #4 share convenient bath.

First Floor	1,824 sq. ft.
Second Floor	1,580 sq. ft.
Total Living Area	3,404 sq. ft.

PRICE CODE: E

CUSTOMIZE IT!

ORDER TOLL FREE 1■800■533■4350   **24-HOUR FAX ORDERING** 1■800■344■4293

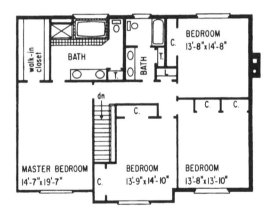

SECOND FLOOR

- BEDROOM 13'-8"x14'-8"
- walk-in closet
- BATH
- BATH
- C.
- dn
- C.
- C.
- MASTER BEDROOM 14'-7"x19'-7"
- BEDROOM 13'-9"x14'-10"
- BEDROOM 13'-8"x13'-10"

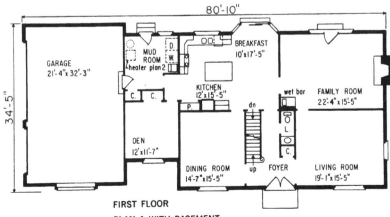

80'-10"

34'-5"

- GARAGE 21'-4"x32'-3"
- MUD ROOM
- heater plan 2
- BREAKFAST 10'x17'-5"
- KITCHEN 12'x15'-5"
- wet bar
- FAMILY ROOM 22'-4"x15'-5"
- DEN 12'x11'-7"
- DINING ROOM 14'-7"x15'-5"
- dn
- up
- FOYER
- LIVING ROOM 19'-1"x15'-5"

FIRST FLOOR
PLAN 1 WITH BASEMENT
PLAN 2 WITHOUT BASEMENT

Contemporary Manor

Features

- Large, comfortable home with plenty of amenities.
- Foyer opens to dining room and living room.
- Family room has a warm fireplace.
- Kitchen with breakfast area features bay window, mud room/laundry area off garage for ultimate convenience.
- First-floor den.
- Second floor has three large bedrooms and a full bath plus a master bedroom with private bath/shower combination.

First Floor	1,868 sq. ft.
Second Floor	1,549 sq. ft.
Total Living Area	3,417 sq. ft.

PRICE CODE: D

PLAN FD8078-L

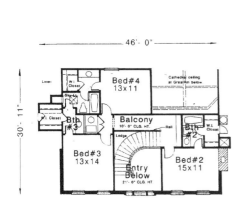

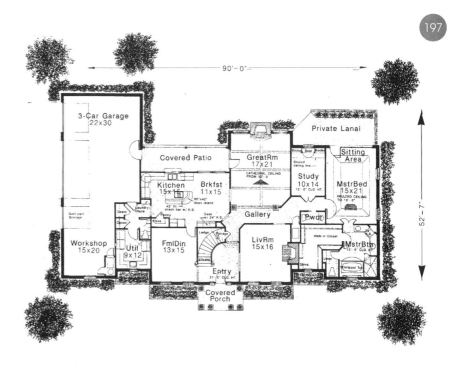

First Floor	2,564 sq. ft.
Second Floor	908 sq. ft.
Total Living Area	3,472 sq. ft.

PRICE CODE: D

CUSTOMIZE IT!

ORDER TOLL FREE   1 ▪ 800 ▪ 533 ▪ 4350   24-HOUR FAX ORDERING   1 ▪ 800 ▪ 344 ▪ 4293

198

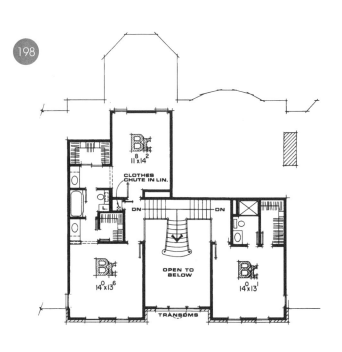

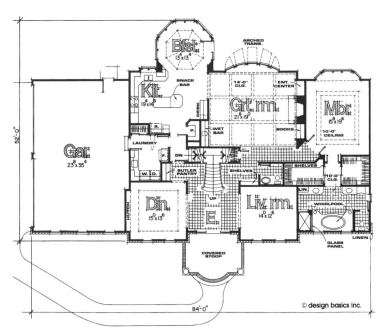

© design basics inc.

Features

- Full 2-story entry graced by large sparkling window and elegant tapering split staircase.
- Formal dining room with special ceiling and hutchspace served by butler pantry.
- Elegant formal living room across entry from dining room extends entertaining options.
- Arched transom windows brighten spacious great room with built-in bookcase, raised hearth fireplace, entertainment center, wet bar and a

14-foot spider-beamed ceiling.
- Pampering luxury bath/dressing area features walk-in closet, his and her vanities and oval whirlpool tub.Comfortable secondary bedrooms, all with walk-in closets; bedrooms #2 and #4 share Hollywood bath.
- Bedroom #3 has its own private bath.
- 4-car garage satisfies many options

First Floor	2,500 sq. ft
Second Floor	973 sq. ft
Total Living Area	3,473 sq. ft

PRICE CODE: E

PLAN CD9112

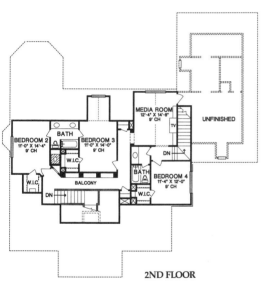

2ND FLOOR

BEDROOM 2
11'-0" X 14'-4"
9' CH

BATH

BEDROOM 3
11'-0" X 14'-0"
9' CH

W.I.C.

W.I.C.

BALCONY

DN

MEDIA ROOM
12'-4" X 14'-8"
9' CH

TV

UNFINISHED

DN

BATH

BEDROOM 4
11'-4" X 12'-0"
9' CH

W.I.C.

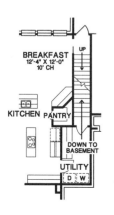

BREAKFAST
12'-4" X 12'-0"
10' CH

UP

KITCHEN

PANTRY

DOWN TO
BASEMENT

UTILITY

D   W

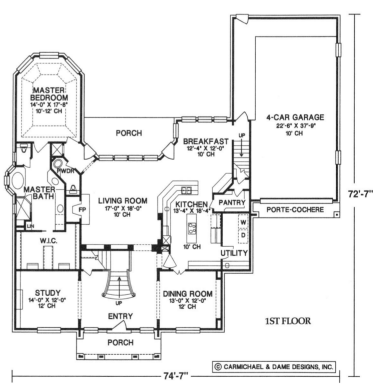

199

MASTER
BEDROOM
14'-0" X 17'-8"
10'-12' CH

PORCH

BREAKFAST
12'-4" X 12'-0"
10' CH

UP

4-CAR GARAGE
22'-6" X 37'-9"
10' CH

PWDR

MASTER
BATH

LIVING ROOM
17'-0" X 18'-0"
10' CH

FP

KITCHEN
13'-4" X 18'-4"

PANTRY

PORTE-COCHERE

W

D

UTILITY

LIN

W.I.C.

10' CH

STUDY
14'-0" X 12'-0"
12' CH

UP

DINING ROOM
13'-0" X 12'-0"
12' CH

ENTRY

72'-7"

1ST FLOOR

PORCH

© CARMICHAEL & DAME DESIGNS, INC.

74'-7"

First Floor	2,289 sq. ft.
Second Floor	1,204 sq. ft.
Total Living Area	3,493 sq. ft.

PRICE CODE: F

200

◀ 71' ▶

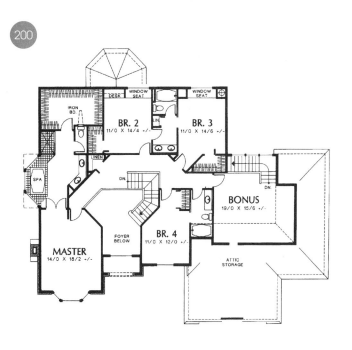

BR. 2
11/0 X 14/4 +/-

BR. 3
11/0 X 14/6 +/-

BONUS
19/0 X 15/6 +/-

BR. 4
11/0 X 12/0 +/-

ATTIC STORAGE

MASTER
14/0 X 18/2 +/-

FOYER BELOW

SPA

IRON BD.

DESK

WINDOW SEAT

WINDOW SEAT

LIN.

LINEN

DN.

DN.

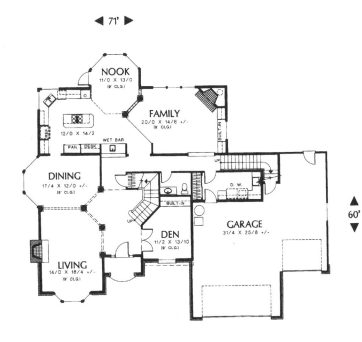

NOOK
11/0 X 13/0
(9' CLG.)

FAMILY
20/0 X 14/6 +/-
(9' CLG.)

12/0 X 14/2

WET BAR

PAN. DESK.

BUILT-IN

DINING
17/4 X 12/0 +/-
(9' CLG.)

DEN
11/2 X 13/10
(9' CLG.)

GARAGE
31/4 X 25/8 +/-

LIVING
14/0 X 18/4 +/-
(9' CLG.)

UP

UP

D. W.

BUILT-IN

REF.

60'

▲
▼

First Floor	1,940 sq. ft.
Second Floor	1,578 sq. ft.
Total Living Area	3,518 sq. ft.
Bonus Room	+292 sq. ft.

PRICE CODE: E

201

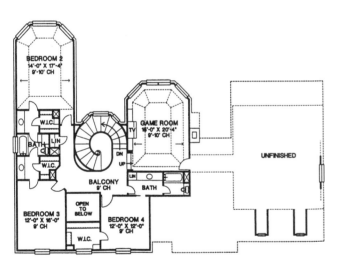

BEDROOM 2
14'-0" X 17'-4"
9'-10" CH

W.I.C.

BATH
LIN

W.I.C.

GAME ROOM
16'-0" X 20'-4"
9'-10" CH

TV

DN
UP

UNFINISHED

BALCONY
9' CH

BATH
LIN

BEDROOM 3
12'-0" X 16'-0"
9' CH

OPEN
TO
BELOW

BEDROOM 4
12'-0" X 12'-0"
9' CH

W.I.C.

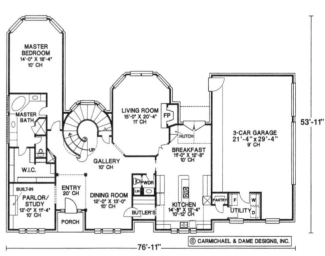

MASTER
BEDROOM
14'-0" X 18'-4"
10' CH

MASTER
BATH

W.I.C.

BUILT-IN
PARLOR/
STUDY
12'-0" X 11'-4"
10' CH

ENTRY
20' CH

PORCH

LIVING ROOM
15'-0" X 20'-4"
11' CH

FP

HUTCH

GALLERY
10' CH

UP

DINING ROOM
12'-0" X 13'-0"
10' CH

PWDR
LIN

BUTLER'S

KITCHEN
14'-8" X 12'-4"
10'-12' CH

BREAKFAST
11'-0" X 12'-8"
10' CH

PANTRY

F

W

UTILITY
D

3-CAR GARAGE
21'-4" X 29'-4"
9' CH

53'-11"

76'-11"

© CARMICHAEL & DAME DESIGNS, INC.

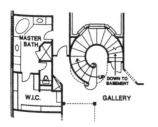

MASTER
BATH

UP
DOWN TO
BASEMENT

W.I.C.

GALLERY

First Floor	2,090 sq. ft.
Second Floor	1,439 sq. ft.
Total Living Area	3,529 sq. ft.

PRICE CODE: F

202

SECOND FLOOR

FIRST FLOOR PLAN 2 WITHOUT BASEMENT

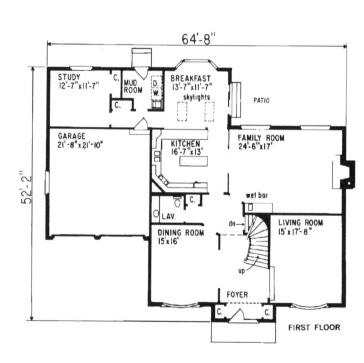

64'-8"

52'-2"

FIRST FLOOR

Natural Elegance

Features

- First floor features a large kitchen with island plus a formal dining room and breakfast nook with skylights.
- Large living and family rooms.

- First floor study.
- First floor lavatory.
- Second floor features three bedrooms plus large master bedroom with private bath.

First Floor	2,007 sq. ft.
Second Floor	1,597 sq. ft.
Total Living Area	3,604 sq. ft.

PRICE CODE: E

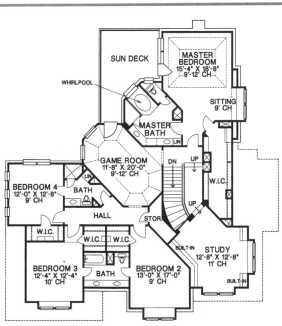

SUN DECK

MASTER BEDROOM
15'-4" X 18'-8"
9'-12' CH

WHIRLPOOL

SITTING
9' CH

MASTER BATH

LIN

UP

W.I.C.

GAME ROOM
11'-8" X 20'-0"
9'-12' CH

DN

UP

BEDROOM 4
12'-0" X 12'-8"
9' CH

BATH

LIN

HALL

STOR.

UP

BUILT-IN

STUDY
12'-8" X 12'-8"
11' CH

W.I.C.

W.I.C.

BEDROOM 3
12'-4" X 12'-4"
10' CH

BATH

BEDROOM 2
13'-0" X 17'-0"
9' CH

BUILT-IN

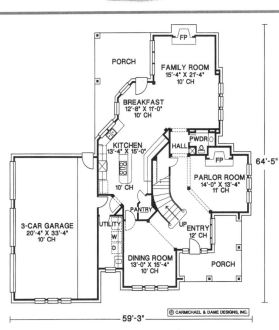

PORCH

FP

FAMILY ROOM
15'-4" X 21'-4"
10' CH

BREAKFAST
12'-8" X 11'-0"
10' CH

KITCHEN
13'-4" X 15'-0"
10' CH

PWDR

HALL

FP

PARLOR ROOM
14'-0" X 13'-4"
11' CH

3-CAR GARAGE
20'-4" X 33'-4"
10' CH

UTILITY

PANTRY

W
D

UP

ENTRY
12' CH

DINING ROOM
13'-0" X 15'-4"
10' CH

PORCH

64'-5"

59'-3"

© CARMICHAEL & DAME DESIGNS, INC.

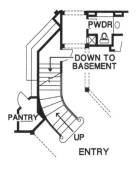

PWDR

DOWN TO BASEMENT

PANTRY

UP

ENTRY

First Floor	1,550 sq. ft.
Second Floor	2,102 sq. ft.
Total Living Area	3,652 sq. ft.

PRICE CODE: F

204

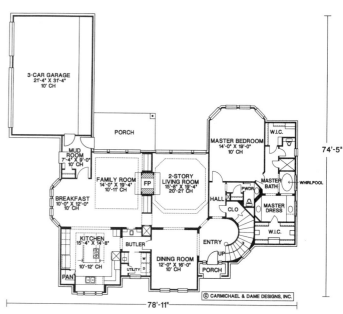

© CARMICHAEL & DAME DESIGNS, INC.

74'-5"

78'-11"

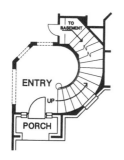

First Floor	2,321 sq. ft.
Second Floor	1,356 sq. ft.
Total Living Area	3,677 sq. ft.

PRICE CODE: F

205

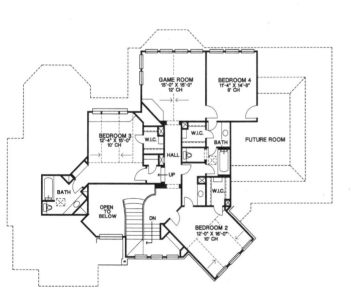

GAME ROOM
15'-0" X 15'-0"
12' CH

BEDROOM 4
11'-4" X 14'-8"
8' CH

BEDROOM 3
12'-4" X 15'-0"
10' CH

W.I.C.

W.I.C.

BATH

FUTURE ROOM

HALL

UP

W.I.C.

BATH

OPEN TO
BELOW

DN

BEDROOM 2
12'-0" X 16'-0"
10' CH

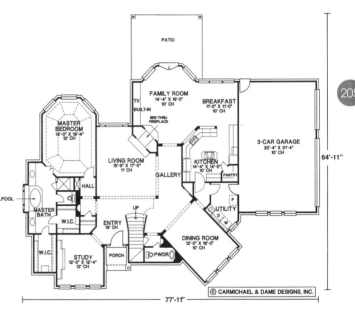

PATIO

FAMILY ROOM
14'-4" X 19'-0"
10' CH

BREAKFAST
11'-0" X 11'-0"
10' CH

TV
BUILT-IN

SEE-THRU
FIREPLACE

3-CAR GARAGE
20'-4" X 31'-4"
10' CH

MASTER
BEDROOM
14'-0" X 19'-4"
12' CH

LIVING ROOM
15'-8" X 17'-0"
11' CH

KITCHEN
14'-4" X 14'-0"
10' CH

GALLERY

PANTRY

POOL

MASTER
BATH

W.I.C.

ENTRY
19' CH

UP

UTILITY

F

D W

W.I.C.

STUDY
12'-0" X 12'-4"
12' CH

PORCH

PWDR

DINING ROOM
12'-0" X 16'-0"
10' CH

© CARMICHAEL & DAME DESIGNS, INC.

64'-11"

77'-11"

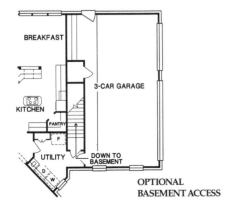

BREAKFAST

3-CAR GARAGE

KITCHEN

PANTRY

F

UTILITY

DOWN TO
BASEMENT

D W

OPTIONAL
BASEMENT ACCESS

First Floor	2,362 sq. ft.
Second Floor	1,319 sq. ft.
Total Living Area	3,681 sq. ft.

PRICE CODE: F

CUSTOMIZE IT!

ORDER TOLL FREE 1■800■533■4350   24-HOUR FAX ORDERING   1■800■344■4293

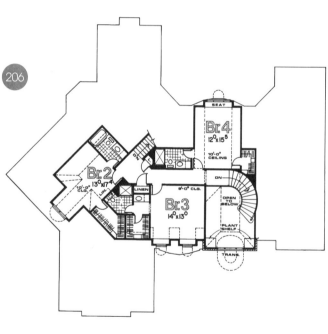

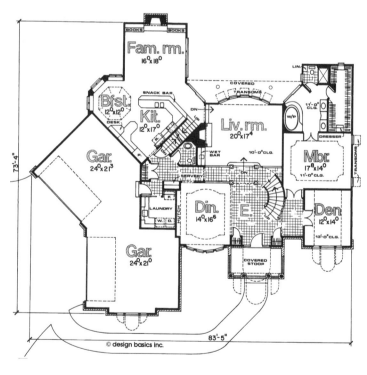

© design basics inc.

Features

- Spectacular volume entry with curving staircase and columns leading into sunken living room.
- Volume living room contains fireplace, bowed window and wet bar.
- Family room to the back with bookcase surrounding fireplace.
- Dramatic kitchen complete with large snack

bar, pantry, and desk is open to family room and bayed dinette with unique ceiling detail.

- 4-car garage.
- Double doors open into volume master suite on main level with private back patio door, oval whirlpool and large walk-incloset.
- Upstairs landing views plant shelves and entry below.

First Floor	**2,617 sq. ft.**
Second Floor	**1,072 sq. ft.**
Total Living Area	**3,689 sq. ft.**

PRICE CODE: F

PLAN CD9104

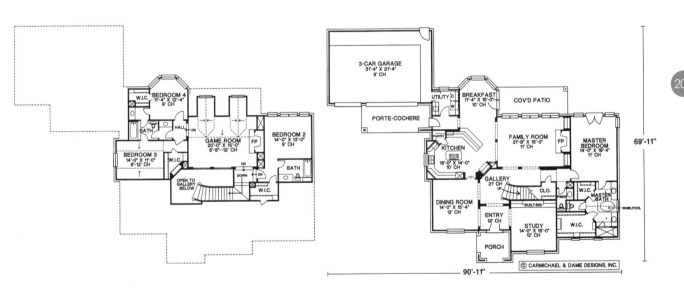

207

BEDROOM 4
11'-4" X 12'-4"
9' CH

GAME ROOM
20'-0" X 15'-0"
6'-8"--12' CH

BEDROOM 2
14'-0" X 13'-0"
9' CH

BEDROOM 3
14'-0" X 11'-0"
9'-12' CH

W.I.C.
BATH
HALL
DN
FP
BATH
OPEN TO GALLERY BELOW
DOWN
DN
W.I.C.

3-CAR GARAGE
31'-4" X 21'-4"
9' CH

UTILITY
BREAKFAST
11'-4" X 15'-0"
10' CH

COV'D PATIO

PORTE-COCHERE

PANTRY
KITCHEN
16'-0" X 14'-0"
10' CH

FAMILY ROOM
21'-8" X 15'-0"
11' CH

FP

MASTER BEDROOM
14'-0" X 19'-4"
11' CH

69'-11"

GALLERY
21' CH
UP
CLO.
W.I.C.
MASTER BATH
WHIRLPOOL

DINING ROOM
14'-0" X 15'-4"
12' CH

BUILT-INS

ENTRY
12' CH

STUDY
14'-0" X 15'-0"
12' CH

W.I.C.

PORCH

© CARMICHAEL & DAME DESIGNS, INC.

90'-11"

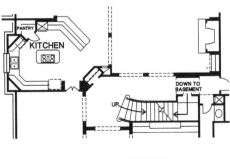

PANTRY
KITCHEN

DOWN TO BASEMENT

UP.

OPTIONAL BASEMENT ACCESS

First Floor	2,350 sq. ft.
Second Floor	1,378 sq. ft.
Total Living Area	3,728 sq. ft.

PRICE CODE: F

CUSTOMIZE IT!

ORDER TOLL FREE 1▪800▪533▪4350 24-HOUR FAX ORDERING 1▪800▪344▪4293

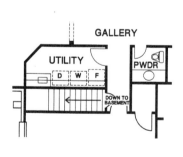

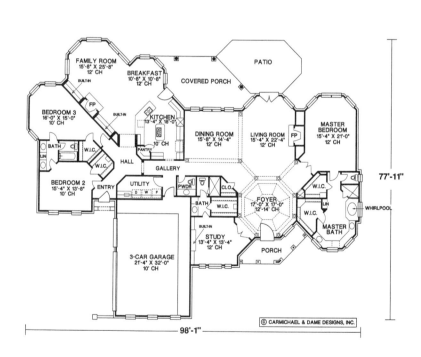

Total Living Area   **3,734 sq. ft.**

PRICE CODE: F

CUSTOMIZE IT!

ORDER TOLL FREE   1∎800∎533∎4350   24-HOUR FAX ORDERING   1∎800∎344∎4293

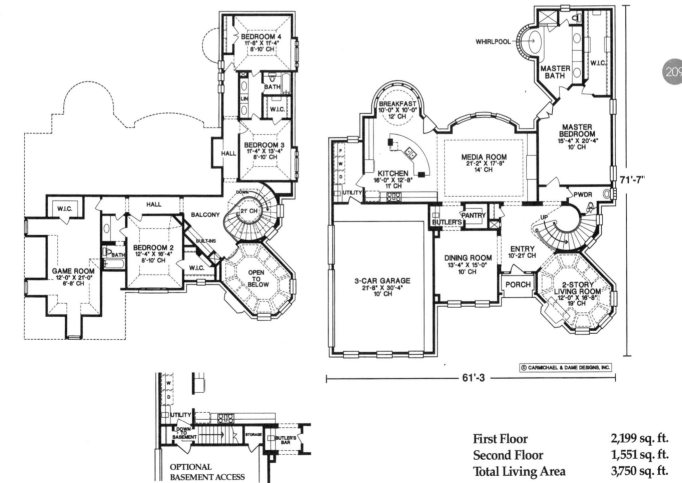

209

BEDROOM 4
11'-8" X 11'-4"
8'-10" CH

BATH

LIN

W.I.C.

HALL

BEDROOM 3
11'-4" X 13'-4"
8'-10" CH

W.I.C.

HALL

BALCONY

DOWN

21' CH

W.I.C.

BATH

BEDROOM 2
12'-4" X 16'-4"
8'-10" CH

BUILT-INS

W.I.C.

GAME ROOM
12'-0" X 21'-0"
6'-8" CH

OPEN TO BELOW

WHIRLPOOL

MASTER BATH

W.I.C.

MASTER BEDROOM
15'-4" X 20'-4"
10' CH

BREAKFAST
10'-0" X 10'-0"
12' CH

MEDIA ROOM
21'-2" X 17'-8"
14' CH

KITCHEN
16'-0" X 12'-8"
11' CH

F
W
D

UTILITY

PWDR

UP

PANTRY

BUTLER'S

DINING ROOM
13'-4" X 15'-0"
10' CH

ENTRY
10'-21' CH

3-CAR GARAGE
21'-8" X 30'-4"
10' CH

PORCH

2-STORY LIVING ROOM
12'-0" X 16'-8"
19' CH

71'-7"

© CARMICHAEL & DAME DESIGNS, INC.

61'-3

W
D

UTILITY

DOWN TO BASEMENT

STORAGE

BUTLER'S BAR

OPTIONAL BASEMENT ACCESS

First Floor	2,199 sq. ft.
Second Floor	1,551 sq. ft.
Total Living Area	3,750 sq. ft.

PRICE CODE: F

CUSTOMIZE IT!

ORDER TOLL FREE   1■800■533■4350   24-HOUR FAX ORDERING   1■800■344■4293

PLAN DB2332

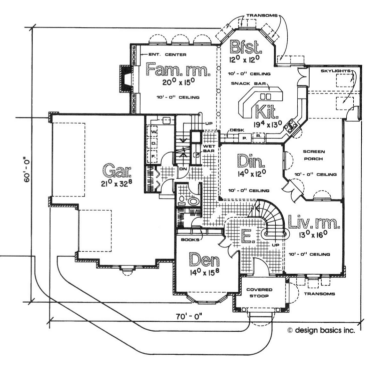

© design basics inc.

Features

- Living room has arched view into screen porch and decorative curved wall.
- Large kitchen with bayed dinette, huge island sink area with raised snack bar, desk and wrapping counters.
- Bedrooms #2 and #3 with walk-in closets share a roomy Hollywood bath.
- Bedroom #4 has private bath and walk-in closet.

- Master bath has walk-in linen storage, glass block wall, whirlpool and his and her vanities with make-up area.
- Sumptuous master suite with see-thru fireplace between sitting room and whirlpool, entertainment center, three built-in dressers and magnificent his and her walk-in closets.

First Floor	1,923 sq. ft.
Second Floor	1,852 sq. ft.
Total Living Area	3,775 sq. ft.

PRICE CODE: F

CUSTOMIZE IT!

ORDER TOLL FREE 1■800■533■4350   24-HOUR FAX ORDERING 1■800■344■4293

211

Hearth and Home

Features

- Open outdoor terrace graces brick exterior across the front.
- Tiled foyer leads to formal master bedroom. In the center is a cathedral-ceiling living room with fireplace and doors leading out to terrace.
- Master bedroom suite includes a brick fireplace, master bath with raised tub and bay window, private toilet, and his/her walk-in closets.
- A library with built-in book shelves is tucked away at the front of the home.
- Three additional bedrooms located upstairs are served by two half baths.

First Floor	**2,868 sq. ft.**
Second Floor	**1,654 sq. ft.**
Total Living Area	**4,522 sq. ft.**

PRICE CODE: E

CUSTOMIZE IT!

ORDER TOLL FREE 1▪800▪533▪4350   24-HOUR FAX ORDERING   1▪800▪344▪4293

PLAN FD8128-L

212

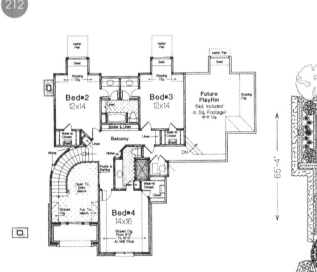

First Floor	2,807 sq. ft.
Second Floor	1,063 sq. ft.
Total Living Area	3,870 sq. ft.

PRICE CODE: E

SECOND FLOOR

Master Bedroom 15' x 16'-10", *Bath*, *skylight*, *upper family room*, *Balcony*, *Bedroom 13' x 12'*, *Bedroom 12' x 11'*, *upper foyer*, *dn*, *Bedroom 15' x 14'-4"*

78'-5" 50'-4"

PATIO · STORAGE · D/W · MUD ROOM · BREAKFAST 16'-6" x 10' snack counter · KITCHEN 15' x 15'-6" · bar · FAMILY ROOM 21' x 26'-6" · PATIO · GARAGE 23'-4" x 30' · BATH · desk · oven · heater clo plan - 2 · logs · book shelves · STUDY 12' x 15'-6" · DINING ROOM 13' x 15'-6" · pantry · dn · up · FOYER · LIVING ROOM 15' x 15'-6"

FIRST FLOOR
PLAN 1 WITH BASEMENT
PLAN 2 WITHOUT BASEMENT

Modern Tudor

Features

- Exciting Tudor adaptation shows interesting roof lines, window treatment, and appealing use of brick and stucco.
- Two-story entrance foyer exhibits the curved staircase to second floor.
- The right wing contains the living room and family room, sharing side-by-side fireplaces.
- Second-floor hall overlooks family room.
- Master bedroom includes walk-in closet and deluxe bath with skylight.
- Three additional bedrooms upstairs share a full bath with double vanity.

First Floor	2,250 sq. ft.
Second Floor	1,632 sq. ft.
Total Living Area	3,882 sq. ft.

PRICE CODE: E

CUSTOMIZE IT!

ORDER TOLL FREE 1■800■533■4350   **24-HOUR FAX ORDERING** 1■800■344■4293

214

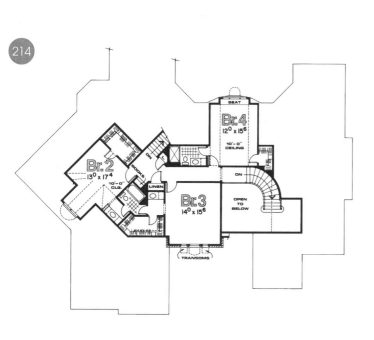

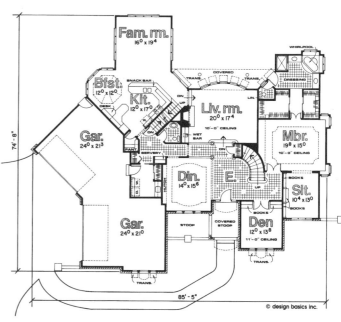

© design basics inc.

Features

- Spectacular entry features dramatic views of living room and dining room areas, as well as balcony above.
- Double doors off entry open to private den with built-in bookshelves.
- Elegant columns accent boundaries of open formal rooms.
- Bowed windows, raised hearth fireplace and wet bar highlight sunken living room.
- Gourmet kitchen includes double oven,

large snack bar, walk-in pantry, built-in desk and lazy Susans.
- Sunny, bayed dinette with vaulted octagon ceiling detail.
- Dressing area has his and her walk-in closet, corner whirlpool, and access to the outside.
- Bedrooms #2 and #3 share Hollywood bath and have private dressing areas.
- Bedroom #4 has private 3/4 bath.

First Floor	**2,813 sq. ft.**
Second Floor	**1,091 sq. ft.**
Total Living Area	**3,904 sq. ft.**

PRICE CODE: F

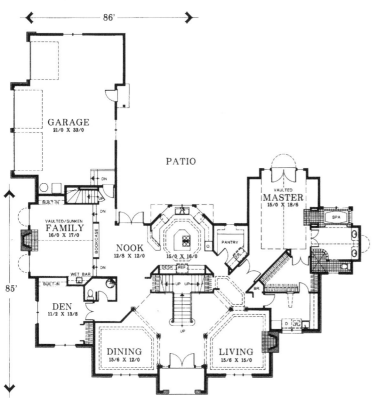

86'

85'

GARAGE
21/0 X 33/0

PATIO

VAULTED
MASTER
15/0 X 18/6

SPA

VAULTED/SUNKEN
FAMILY
16/0 X 17/0

NOOK
12/8 X 12/0

PANTRY

WET BAR

DEN
11/2 X 13/8

DESK
REF

UP   UP

BR.

DINING
15/6 X 12/0

LIVING
15/6 X 15/0

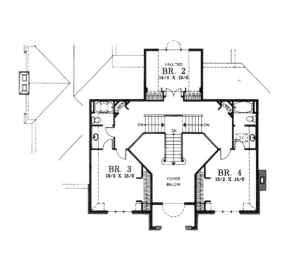

VAULTED
BR. 2
14/4 X 10/0

BR. 3
13/2 X 15/0

BR. 4
13/2 X 15/0

FOYER
BELOW

215

First Floor	2,870 sq. ft.
Second Floor	1,075 sq. ft.
Total Living Area	3,945 sq. ft.

PRICE CODE: E

PLAN DB2016

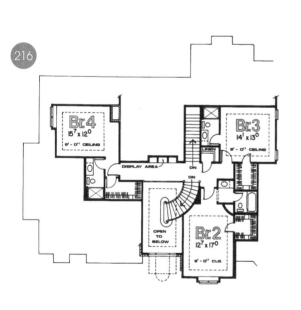

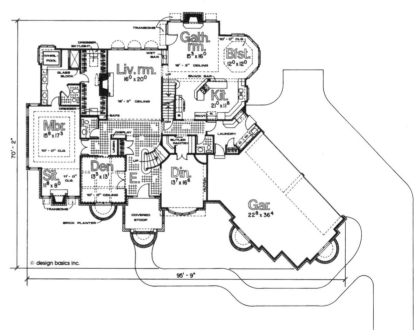

Features

- Spectacular 2-story-high entry showcases floating, curved staircase.
- Specialty windows throughout.
- Butler pantry for formal serving into dining room with hutch space.
- Fashionable built-in shelving and cabinetry.
- Side utility entrance separate from 4-car garage.
- 3 fireplace locations.
- Repetitive arched windows at back of volume living room.

- Gourmet kitchen with cooktop in ,island, snack bar, pantry and desk.
- Luxurious master suite features tiered ceiling and warm sitting room with fireplace.
- Pampering master bath/dressing area boasts double vanities, glass block walls at corner whirlpool and separate shower, huge walk-in closet with built-in dressers, tunneled skylight and an iron-a-way.
- Convenient family staircase at the back.

First Floor	**2,839 sq. ft.**
Second Floor	**1,111 sq. ft.**
Total Living Area	**3,950 sq. ft.**

PRICE CODE: F

CUSTOMIZE IT!

ORDER TOLL FREE 1■800■533■4350 **24-HOUR FAX ORDERING** 1■800■344■4293

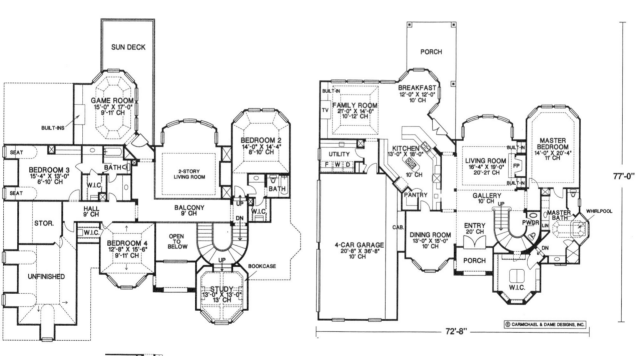

SUN DECK

GAME ROOM
15'-0" X 17'-0"
9'-11" CH

BUILT-INS

BEDROOM 2
14'-0" X 14'-4"
8'-10" CH

SEAT

BATH

2-STORY
LIVING ROOM

BEDROOM 3
15'-4" X 13'-0"
6'-10" CH

W.I.C

BATH

SEAT

HALL
9' CH

BALCONY
9' CH

W.I.C

STOR.

W.I.C

BEDROOM 4
12'-8" X 15'-6"
9'-11" CH

OPEN
TO
BELOW

UP
DN

UNFINISHED

UP

BOOKCASE

STUDY
13'-0" X 13'-0"
13' CH

PORCH

BUILT-IN

FAMILY ROOM
21'-0" X 14'-0"
10'-12" CH

BREAKFAST
12'-0" X 12'-0"
10' CH

TV

UTILITY

KITCHEN
13'-0" X 18'-0"
10' CH

MASTER
BEDROOM
14'-0" X 20'-4"
11' CH

LIVING ROOM
16'-4" X 19'-0"
20'-21' CH

BUILT-IN

FP

F W D

PANTRY

BUILT-IN

GALLERY
10' CH

UP

4-CAR GARAGE
20'-8" X 36'-8"
10' CH

CAB.

DINING ROOM
13'-0" X 15'-0"
10' CH

ENTRY
20' CH

PWDR

LIN

MASTER
BATH

WHIRLPOOL

DN

PORCH

W.I.C

© CARMICHAEL & DAME DESIGNS, INC.

77'-0"

72'-8"

217

UTILITY

F W D

KITCHEN
13'-0" X 18'-0"
10' CH

STOR.

PANTRY

DOWN
TO
BASEMENT

CAB.

4-CAR GARAGE
36'-6" X 21'-8"
10' CH

First Floor   2,489 sq. ft.
Second Floor   1,650 sq. ft.
Total Living Area   4,139 sq. ft.

PRICE CODE: F

PLAN CD9119

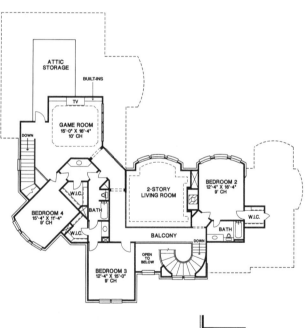

218

ATTIC STORAGE

BUILT-INS

TV

GAME ROOM
15'-0" X 18'-4"
10' CH

DOWN

W.I.C.

BEDROOM 4
15'-4" X 11'-4"
9' CH

BATH

W.I.C.

2-STORY LIVING ROOM

BEDROOM 2
12'-4" X 16'-4"
9' CH

W.I.C.

BATH

BALCONY

OPEN TO BELOW

DOWN

BEDROOM 3
12'-4" X 15'-0"
9' CH

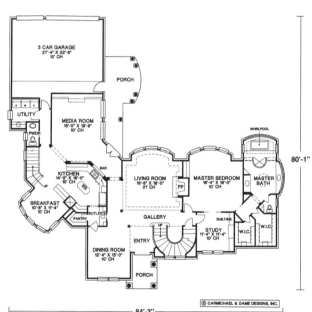

3 CAR GARAGE
27'-4" X 22'-8"
10' CH

PORCH

UTILITY

PWDR

MEDIA ROOM
15'-0" X 19'-8"
10' CH

KITCHEN
14'-0" X 16'-0"
10' CH

BAR

BREAKFAST
10'-8" X 11'-4"
10' CH

UP

BUTLER

PANTRY

LIVING ROOM
18'-8" X 18'-0"
21' CH

FP

MASTER BEDROOM
16'-4" X 18'-0"
10' CH

WHIRLPOOL

MASTER BATH

GALLERY

BUILT-INS

W.I.C.

W.I.C.

DINING ROOM
12'-4" X 15'-0"
10' CH

ENTRY

UP

STUDY
11'-4" X 11'-4"
10' CH

PORCH

© CARMICHAEL & DAME DESIGNS, INC.

80'-1"

84'-3"

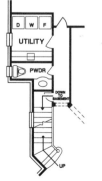

D W F

UTILITY

PWDR

DOWN TO BASEMENT

UP

First Floor	2,688 sq. ft.
Second Floor	1,540 sq. ft.
Total Living Area	4,228 sq. ft.

PRICE CODE: F

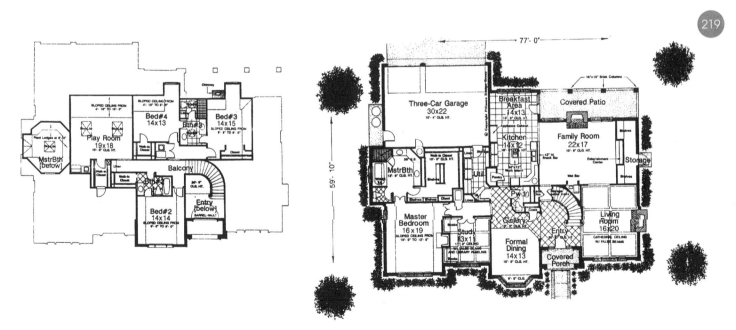

First Floor	2,761 sq. ft.
Second Floor	1,514 sq. ft.
Total Living Area	4,275 sq. ft.

PRICE CODE: F

PLAN CD9111

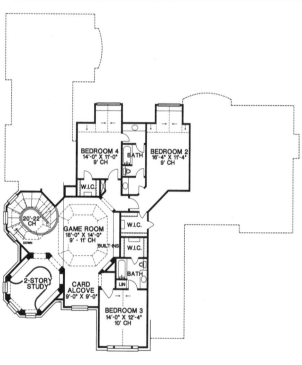

BEDROOM 4
14'-0" X 11'-0"
9' CH

BEDROOM 2
16'-4" X 11'-4"
9' CH

BATH

W.I.C.

20'-22
CH

GAME ROOM
18'-0" X 14'-0"
9' - 11' CH
[BUILT-INS]

W.I.C.

W.I.C.

DOWN

2-STORY
STUDY

CARD
ALCOVE
9'-0" X 9'-0"

BATH

LIN

BEDROOM 3
14'-0" X 12'-4"
10' CH

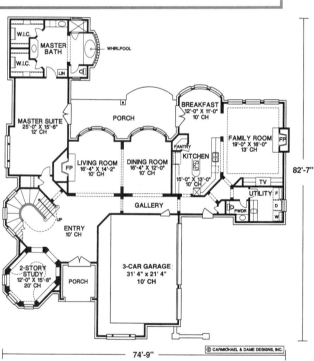

W.I.C.

MASTER
BATH

W.I.C.

LIN

WHIRLPOOL

MASTER SUITE
25'-0" X 15'-6"
12' CH

PORCH

BREAKFAST
12'-0" X 11'-0"
10' CH

FAMILY ROOM
19'-0" X 16'-0"
13' CH

FP

FP

LIVING ROOM
16'-4" X 14'-2"
10' CH

DINING ROOM
16'-4" X 12'-0"
10' CH

PANTRY

KITCHEN

15'-0" X 13'-0"
10' CH

TV

UTILITY

UP

ENTRY
10' CH

GALLERY

PWDR

2-STORY
STUDY
12'-0" X 15'-8"
20' CH

PORCH

3-CAR GARAGE
31' 4" X 21' 4"
10' CH

82'-7"

74'-9"

© CARMICHAEL & DAME DESIGNS, INC.

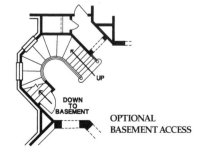

DOWN
TO
BASEMENT

UP

OPTIONAL
BASEMENT ACCESS

First Floor	2,788 sq. ft.
Second Floor	1,527 sq. ft.
Total Living Area	4,315 sq. ft.

PRICE CODE: F

CUSTOMIZE IT!

ORDER TOLL FREE **1 ▪ 800 ▪ 533 ▪ 4350**   24-HOUR FAX ORDERING **1 ▪ 800 ▪ 344 ▪ 4293**

PLAN CD9153

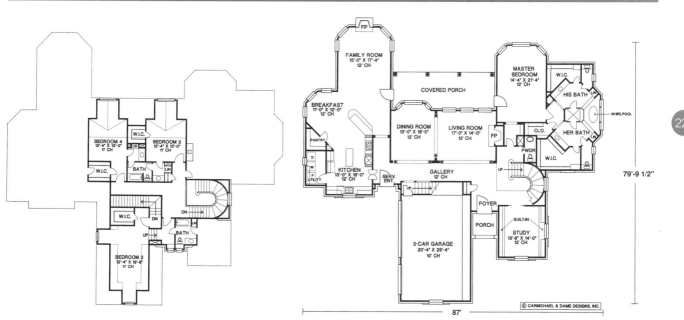

221

FAMILY ROOM
15'-0" X 17'-4"
12' CH

COVERED PORCH

MASTER BEDROOM
14'-4" X 21'-4"
12' CH

W.I.C.

HIS BATH

WHIRLPOOL

HER BATH

BREAKFAST
11'-0" X 12'-0"
12' CH

DINING ROOM
13'-0" X 16'-0"
12' CH

LIVING ROOM
17'-0" X 14'-0"
12' CH

FP

CLO.

PANTRY

PWDR

W.I.C.

KITCHEN
13'-0" X 18'-0"
12' CH

UTILITY

SERV. ENT

GALLERY
12' CH

UP

79'-9 1/2"

FOYER

PORCH

BUILT-IN

STUDY
13'-8" X 14'-0"
12' CH

3-CAR GARAGE
20'-4" X 29'-4"
10' CH

© CARMICHAEL & DAME DESIGNS, INC.

87'

BEDROOM 4
12'-4" X 13'-0"
11' CH

W.I.C.

BEDROOM 3
12'-4" X 13'-0"
11' CH

BATH

LIN

W.I.C.

W.I.C.

DN

DN

UP

BATH

BEDROOM 2
12'-4" X 19'-8"
11' CH

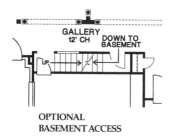

GALLERY
12' CH

DOWN TO BASEMENT

UP

**OPTIONAL
BASEMENT ACCESS**

First Floor   3,026 sq. ft.
Second Floor   1,377 sq. ft.
Total Living Area   4,403 sq. ft.

PRICE CODE: F

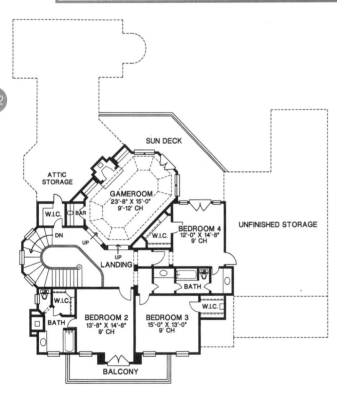

SUN DECK

ATTIC STORAGE

GAMEROOM
23'-8" X 15'-0"
9'-12' CH

BEDROOM 4
12'-0" X 14'-8"
9' CH

UNFINISHED STORAGE

W.I.C.

BAR

DN

UP

UP

LANDING

W.I.C.

BATH

BEDROOM 2
13'-8" X 14'-8"
9' CH

BEDROOM 3
15'-0" X 13'-0"
9' CH

W.I.C.

BATH

W.I.C.

BALCONY

222

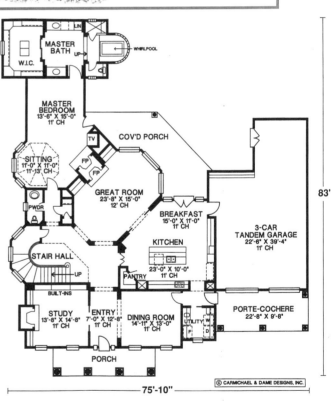

MASTER BATH

W.I.C.

LIN

UP

WHIRLPOOL

MASTER BEDROOM
13'-6" X 15'-0"
11' CH

COV'D PORCH

TV

FP

FP

SITTING
11'-0" X 11'-0"
11'-13' CH

PWDR

GREAT ROOM
23'-8" X 15'-0"
12' CH

BREAKFAST
15'-0" X 11'-0"
11' CH

3-CAR TANDEM GARAGE
22'-6" X 39'-4"
11' CH

KITCHEN
23'-0" X 10'-0"
11' CH

STAIR HALL

UP

PANTRY

BUILT-INS

STUDY
13'-8" X 14'-8"
11' CH

ENTRY
7'-0" X 12'-8"
11' CH

DINING ROOM
14'-11" X 13'-0"
11' CH

UTILITY

PORTE-COCHERE
22'-8" X 9'-8"

PORCH

83'

75'-10"

© CARMICHAEL & DAME DESIGNS, INC.

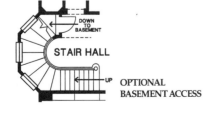

DOWN TO BASEMENT

STAIR HALL

UP

OPTIONAL BASEMENT ACCESS

First Floor   2,728 sq. ft.
Second Floor   1,617 sq. ft.
Total Living Area 4,345 sq. ft.

PRICE CODE: F

CUSTOMIZE IT!

ORDER TOLL FREE **1■800■533■4350**   24-HOUR FAX ORDERING **1■800■344■4293**

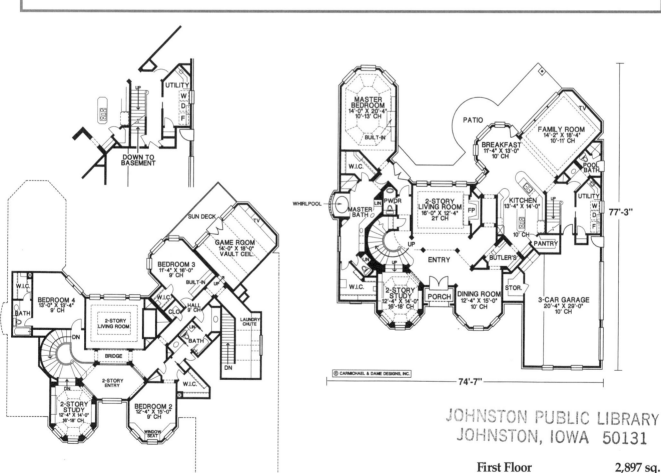

223

JOHNSTON PUBLIC LIBRARY
JOHNSTON, IOWA 50131

First Floor	2,897 sq. ft.
Second Floor	1,603 sq. ft.
Total Living Area	4,500 sq. ft.

PRICE CODE: F

CUSTOMIZE IT!

ORDER TOLL FREE   1•800•533•4350   24-HOUR FAX ORDERING   1•800•344•4293

224

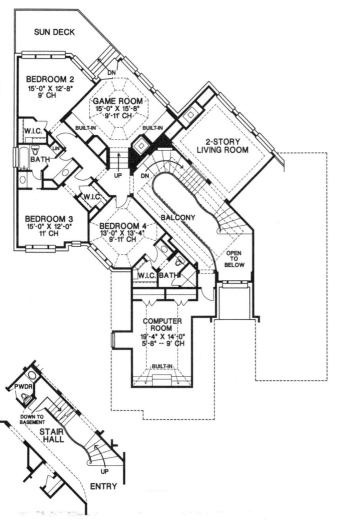

SUN DECK

BEDROOM 2
15'-0" X 12'-8"
9' CH

W.I.C.

BATH
LIN

BEDROOM 3
15'-0" X 12'-0"
11' CH

W.I.C.

DN

GAME ROOM
15'-0" X 15'-8"
9'-11' CH

BUILT-IN
BUILT-IN

UP
DN

2-STORY
LIVING ROOM

BALCONY

BEDROOM 4
13'-0" X 13'-4"
9'-11' CH

W.I.C. BATH

OPEN TO
BELOW

COMPUTER
ROOM
19'-4" X 14'-0"
5'-8" -- 9' CH

BUILT-IN

PWDR

DOWN TO
BASEMENT

STAIR
HALL

UP

ENTRY

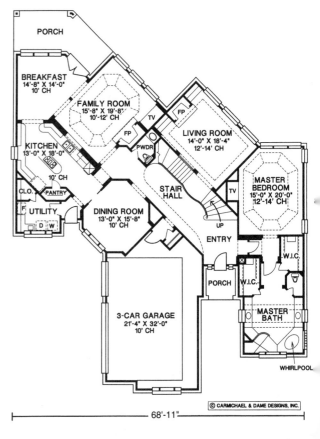

PORCH

BREAKFAST
14'-8" X 14'-0"
10' CH

FAMILY ROOM
15'-8" X 19'-8"
10'-12' CH

TV

FP

FP

LIVING ROOM
14'-0" X 18'-4"
12'-14' CH

KITCHEN
13'-0" X 18'-0"
10' CH

PWDR

STAIR
HALL

TV

MASTER
BEDROOM
15'-0" X 20'-0"
12'-14' CH

CLO.

PANTRY

UTILITY

D   W

DINING ROOM
13'-0" X 15'-8"
10' CH

UP

ENTRY

W.I.C.

3-CAR GARAGE
21'-4" X 32'-0"
10' CH

PORCH

W.I.C.

MASTER
BATH

WHIRLPOOL

© CARMICHAEL & DAME DESIGNS, INC.

|— 68'-11" —|

First Floor	2,725 sq. ft.
Second Floor	1,788 sq. ft.
Total Living Area	4,513 sq. ft.

PRICE CODE: F